THE HIDDEN ENEMIES OF THE PRIESTHOOD

THE HIDDEN ENEMIES OF THE PRIESTHOOD

The Contributions of St. Thomas Aquinas

BASIL COLE, OP

ST PAULS

Library of Congress Cataloging-in-Publication Data

Cole, Basil.
  The hidden enemies of the priesthood : the contributions of St. Thomas
Aquinas / Basil Cole.
    p. cm.
  ISBN 0-8189-1226-X
1. Catholic Church—Clergy—Religious life. 2. Deadly sins. 3. Thomas, Aquinas,
Saint, 1225?-1274. I. Title.

BX1912.5.C55 2006
248.38'92—dc22

                           2005029121

Imprimi Potest:
V. Rev. D. Dominic Izzo, O.P., Prior Provincial
Province of St. Joseph

Nihil Obstat:
Rev. Giles Dimock, O.P.
Censor Deputatus

Imprimatur:
Rev. Msgr. Godfrey Mosley
Vicar General for the Archdiocese of Washington
June 3, 2005

The Nihil Obstat and Imprimatur are official declarations
that a book or pamphlet is free of doctrinal or moral
error. No implication is contained therein that those
who have granted the Nihil Obstat and Imprimatur agree
with the contents, opinions or statements expressed.

Produced and designed in the United States of America by the
Fathers and Brothers of the Society of St. Paul,
2187 Victory Boulevard, Staten Island, New York 10314-6603,
as part of their communications apostolate.

ISBN 0-8189-1226-X
ISBN 978-0-8189-1226-9

Printing Information:

Current Printing - first digit   1   2   3   4   5   6   7   8   9   10

Year of Current Printing - first year shown

2007   2008   2009   2010   2011   2012   2013   2014   2015

Acknowledgments

Articles on humility and the spirituality of study by Basil Cole, OP, originally published in *Homiletic and Pastoral Review* have been revised for this work and are used with permission.

Occasional citations of the Catechism are from the English translation of the *Catechism of the Catholic Church* for the United States of America copyright © 1994 United States Catholic Conference, Inc. — Libreria Editrice Vaticana.

The translations of brief passages from St. Thomas Aquinas' *Summa Theologiae* are from the Blackfriars/McGraw-Hill edition done in the 1960-1970's under the overall editorship of Thomas Gilby.

The translation of brief passages from St. Thomas Aquinas' *De Malo* is from *On Evil*, Jean Oesterle, tr. (Notre Dame, IN: University of Notre Dame Press, 1995).

Table of Contents

Preface

Father Basil Cole, in his book, *The Hidden Enemies of the Priesthood*, discusses the pitfalls of the neglect of the spiritual life in the formation of clergy. Responding to the Second Vatican Council's call, as well as that of *Pastores Dabo Vobis*, Father Cole turns to the theology of St. Thomas Aquinas, to explain the foes of the spiritual life, especially in the light of Thomas' discussion of the seven capital vices.

The Second Vatican Council Decree on the Life and Ministry of Priests (*Presbyterorum Ordinis*) taught that through the sacrament of Holy Orders, priests "...by the anointing of the Holy Spirit, are signed with a special character and are conformed to Christ the Priest in such a way that they can act in the person of Christ the Head" (PO 2). This teaching is more fully expressed in both the 1992 Post Synodal Apostolic Exhortation, *Pastores Dabo Vobis*, and in the 1994 *Catechism of the Catholic Church*. In order for a priest to fully embrace the call given to him, his spiritual life must be at the heart of his formation. The Council pointed out in its decree, *Optatam Totius* that "...students must learn to live in intimate and unceasing union with God the Father through his Son Jesus Christ in the Holy Spirit" (OT 8).

While the Council taught clearly the essential uniqueness of the ministerial priesthood and the need for strong spiritual formation, the teaching unfortunately was not fully heeded. Father Cole calls us to return to the Council, the recent magisterium of the Church, and the theology of Thomas and the Fathers in order to recover the richness of spiritual formation articulated by the teaching.

A priest is first and foremost called to give his life completely to Jesus Christ and the Church in service to the People of God. To do this he must follow the Lord to the point of leaving everything (Lk 5:11) and laying down his life for others (Jn 15:13). The priest, in pastoral charity, gives himself as a total self gift to Christ and to the Church, most especially the people he serves. He is, therefore, first and foremost to be a man with the heart of Christ (PDV 49), who experiences in his own heart the love the Father has for him as beloved son in the Holy Spirit.

The priest too must be prepared for spiritual combat and expect to encounter the same temptations as Christ. The temptations will take a different form today but have the same purpose, to drive a wedge between the Father and his chosen son. Furthermore, the priest, as Father Cole notes, is not to be duped by modern disbelief in the evil one. Rather he must understand that evil exists. The father of lies will try to seduce him and move him away from intimacy with the triune God and away from pastoral charity. The priest is to take seriously in his heart the words of the Our Father, "deliver us from evil," trusting that the Father will open his eyes to recognize evil and protect him.

Through the words of Thomas Aquinas, those of the Fathers of the Church and the *Catechism of the Catholic Church*, Father Cole provides a most helpful presentation for bishops, priests and seminarians on the vices clergy face today. His discussion is thorough and helps to alert us to not only the evident ways but also the hidden ways in which we can fall into the seven capital vices of pride, avarice, envy, anger, lust, gluttony and acedia as well as those of vainglory and ambition. He also provides helps for overcoming the vices when we become aware of them in our lives.

This book will serve as an examination of conscience and hopefully lead clergy who read it to conversion and deeper intimacy with the Father, Son and Holy Spirit. For the lay faithful, it will help them to understand better the meaning of the priesthood as well as the temptations priests face today. It will also assist them to understand the temptations and vices they may face in their spiritual lives.

Countering any vice requires prayer, true self-knowledge before God, and the grace of humility to receive all that the Triune God offers to us. The priest recognizes in Mary, the mother of priests, her virtues of docility, receptivity, obedience and humility. As a man of prayer, the priest is to pray for these virtues, as well as the stirring into flame (2 Tm 1:6) of the gifts he has received from the Holy Spirit in his baptism, confirmation and the sacrament of Holy Orders. Through the intercession of Mary, I pray that as clergy and seminarians read this book that they may come to recognize the hidden enemies of the priesthood in themselves and confidently bring them to the Father so that they may be delivered of them and thus have the heart of Jesus Christ, the Head, Shepherd and Spouse of the Church!

Bishop Samuel J. Aquila
Bishop of Fargo

Introduction

Notwithstanding the papacy of Pope John Paul the Great, priestly defections in the sacred ministry have taken place in the West at an alarming rate. This is not due to lack of grace but lack of personal prudence or management of one's spiritual life.

First, in the initial stages of priestly formation, a vision of the priesthood at times was based upon what the priest simply **does** to the detriment of what he **is**. Second, living in an atmosphere of dissent and doubt concerning the truth of the Catholic faith created a situation where living the dogmas became very weakened if not sometimes seemingly impossible because of a lack of intelligent conviction. Why be convinced of the truth of the Catholic teaching, if it is merely composed of probable and pious opinions about Jesus together with a relativist moral doctrine? Third, if the core of Catholic thought was in flux during seminary training, then the hidden enemies of the priesthood would remain unknown and when they emerged, they would catch the young or middle-aged priest off his guard. Throughout the seventies, eighties and until the two magnificent encyclical letters of John Paul, *Evangelium Vitae* and *Veritatis Splendor*, the doctrinal, liturgical and governmental problems of bishops tended to make the morale of many dioceses dip to low points. Only those priests who were living a very deep spiritual life would come through the varying crises because of their love and trust in the loving providence of the Risen Lord.

Liturgical abuses with the collusion of some bishops led priests and the laity to believe that the Eucharist could be created at the will of the priest and his liturgical committee. Creating his own sweet bread, using unauthorized wine, changing the words of institution, ridiculing the rosary led to a series of misfortunate consequences in the life of the parish such as losing the youth, others no longer coming to Sunday Mass, and the devaluation of the sacrament of penance. Hence the reason for writing this book became very important to me.

St. Thomas Aquinas, the Common Doctor of the Church and the only one named both in the Second Vatican Council and the *Code of Canon Law* remarks that the capital vices contain all the moral vices in principle. So often, however, ignorance of these vices, have led to many shocks and surprises to the sometime over-worked priest. Often, these vices became an unconscious motivating power in the priest's life. Prayer and contemplation would be abandoned for more apostolic activities because the priest would be suffering from either large doses of vainglory, or would be looking for excessive affirmation from his people or his fellow peers in the priesthood. Likewise, apostolic workaholism could have been the bitter fruits of acedia, that repulsion which can take place over spiritual realities and a corresponding failure to face one's inner weaknesses and do something about them with the help of God's grace.

Ignorance of the capital vices which potentially lurk in the depths of the soul was a major disaster ready to happen from the sex abuse cases to the temptations of doubt and even despair about the integrity of the Catholic Church. It takes great and heroic faith to believe that the Catholic Church is truly one, holy, Catholic and apostolic founded by Jesus Christ, true God and true man if the priest is weak-willed, ill equipped intellectually, and bishops fail to lead by correction, or praise of excellence and fidelity.

The purpose of this study is to help the priest and seminarian to be able to reckon with the trials which will occur throughout his life so that he will not be taken aback by the consequences of the capital vices. Because of original sin, feelings tend to replace right reason and faith when making personal decisions about one's personal life and pastoral commitment to lead others to heaven. Ignorance can also do its damage when emotions are repressed or denied, for all the capital vices revolve around unreasonable and ill-formed emotions, as we shall see.

I wish to thank Frs. Giles Dimock, O.P., Juan-Diego Brunetta, O.P. for their timely corrections of the text. Also my gratitude goes out to Fr. Michael Carey, O.P. who together with myself crafted part of an earlier version of Chapter One.

Biblical Abbreviations

OLD TESTAMENT

Genesis	Gn	Nehemiah	Ne	Baruch	Ba
Exodus	Ex	Tobit	Tb	Ezekiel	Ezk
Leviticus	Lv	Judith	Jdt	Daniel	Dn
Numbers	Nb	Esther	Est	Hosea	Ho
Deuteronomy	Dt	1 Maccabees	1 M	Joel	Jl
Joshua	Jos	2 Maccabees	2 M	Amos	Am
Judges	Jg	Job	Jb	Obadiah	Ob
Ruth	Rt	Psalms	Ps	Jonah	Jon
1 Samuel	1 S	Proverbs	Pr	Micah	Mi
2 Samuel	2 S	Ecclesiastes	Ec	Nahum	Na
1 Kings	1 K	Song of Songs	Sg	Habakkuk	Hab
2 Kings	2 K	Wisdom	Ws	Zephaniah	Zp
1 Chronicles	1 Ch	Sirach	Si	Haggai	Hg
2 Chronicles	2 Ch	Isaiah	Is	Malachi	Ml
Ezra	Ezr	Jeremiah	Jr	Zechariah	Zc
		Lamentations	Lm		

NEW TESTAMENT

Matthew	Mt	Ephesians	Eph	Hebrews	Heb
Mark	Mk	Philippians	Ph	James	Jm
Luke	Lk	Colossians	Col	1 Peter	1 P
John	Jn	1 Thessalonians	1 Th	2 Peter	2 P
Acts	Ac	2 Thessalonians	2 Th	1 John	1 Jn
Romans	Rm	1 Timothy	1 Tm	2 John	2 Jn
1 Corinthians	1 Cor	2 Timothy	2 Tm	3 John	3 Jn
2 Corinthians	2 Cor	Titus	Tt	Jude	Jude
Galatians	Gal	Philemon	Phm	Revelation	Rv

Chapter One

The Catholic Priesthood

To begin our theological journey into the Catholic priesthood, it is helpful to read, first of all, two most prominent and profoundly inspiring quotations. They should help us begin our reflections on the Catholic priesthood, and are found in the *Catechism of the Catholic Church*:

> 1589. Before the grandeur of the priestly grace and office, the holy doctors felt an urgent call to conversion in order to conform their whole lives to him whose sacrament had made them ministers. Thus St. Gregory of Nazianzus, as a very young priest, exclaimed:
>
>> We must begin by purifying ourselves before purifying others; we must be instructed to be able to instruct, become light to illuminate, draw close to God to bring him close to others, be sanctified to sanctify, lead by the hand and counsel prudently. I know whose ministers we are, where we find ourselves and to where we strive. I know God's greatness and man's weakness, but also his potential. Who then is the priest? He is the defender of truth, who stands with angels, gives glory with archangels, causes sacrifices to rise to the altar on high, shares Christ's priesthood, refashions creation, restores it in God's image, recreates it for the world on high and, even greater, is divinized and divinizes. [82]

1

And the holy Cure of Ars: "The priest continues the work of redemption on earth.... If we really understood the priest on earth, we would die not of fright but of love.... The Priesthood is the love of the heart of Jesus."[83]

Such awesome and arousing words from two saints should lead us to wonder at the faith mystery of the human person who is given this gift of the Holy Spirit.

The grace and character of Holy Orders given to the priest, the second rank of Holy Orders as we shall see, penetrates and directly consecrates his entire being for intimacy with Jesus Christ and for service and mission to his Church. These two dimensions supplement each other for the priest's task is to mediate between God and the world. He must strive to bring the gifts of God to others, and also to bring man's gifts to God. He officially celebrates the liturgy and ministers the sacraments and sacramentals of the Church to the people. More, he witnesses by his life what it means to be a friend of the Lord Jesus.

What Is Liturgy?

There is no better way to understand the teaching of the Church on the Catholic priesthood than by first examining what the Church teaches regarding the liturgy. From that perspective, we will be in a better position to clarify the role and life of the Catholic priest.

In the *Catechism*, called by our Holy Father John Paul II, "a sure norm for teaching the faith" (CCC 3), we find a very ample explanation of the word "liturgy" for our purposes:

1070. In the New Testament the word "liturgy" refers not only to the celebration of divine worship but also to the proclamation of the Gospel and to active charity. In all of these situations it is a question of the service of God and neighbor. In a liturgical celebration the Church is servant in the image of her Lord, the one "*leitourgos*";[7] she shares in Christ's priesthood (worship), which is both prophetic (proclamation) and kingly (service of charity).

The reader will notice, the Church describes herself (that is, all of the faithful: priests and people) as a servant that shares in Christ's priesthood or worship, which is also prophetic and kingly. Continuing in the same passage, the *Catechism* amplifies the meaning of Christ's priesthood:

> The liturgy then is rightly seen as an exercise of the priestly office of Jesus Christ. It involves the presentation of man's sanctification under the guise of signs perceptible by the senses and its accomplishment in ways appropriate to each of these signs. In it full public worship is performed by the Mystical Body of Jesus Christ, that is, by the Head and his members. From this it follows that every liturgical celebration, because it is an action of Christ the priest and of his Body which is the Church, is a sacred action surpassing all others. No other action of the Church can equal its efficacy by the same title and to the same degree.

It is to be noticed and underscored that the liturgy as public worship is one act, but under two aspects: an act of Christ's priestly office and the act of his Body the Church, his members. And, while this act transcends time and space and surpasses all actions within the Church, and is called a kind of summit (CCC 1074) following the Council's document on the liturgy, the *Catechism* cautions us:

> 1072. "The sacred liturgy does not exhaust the entire activity of the Church" (SC 9); it must be preceded by evangelization, faith, and conversion. It can then

produce its fruits in the lives of the faithful: new life in the Spirit, involvement in the mission of the Church, and service to her unity.

Already, it is clear that just administering the sacraments is not enough. There is a need for preparation, faith/conversion, and a sense of mission and service. From this it is easy to deduce that there must be inspiration, organization and leadership from someone who is authorized to do all this work of the Spirit. Such a thrust had to come from a deep and personal decision of the Lord Jesus so that his plans would be kept intact and vibrate in people's lives throughout all the ages.

Jesus Christ the Priest

Before we try to understand the faith mystery of the Catholic priesthood, we must realize that Jesus Christ, the author of the Catholic priesthood, was himself a priest, the great high priest. What did he do? The *Catechism* puts it beautifully although it needs to be read several times for us to assimilate its full meaning into our minds and memories:

> 1085. In the liturgy of the Church, it is principally his own Paschal mystery that Christ signifies and makes present. During his earthly life Jesus announced his Paschal mystery by his teaching and anticipated it by his actions. When his Hour comes, he lives out the unique event of history which does not pass away: Jesus dies, is buried, rises from the dead, and is seated at the right hand of the Father "once for all" [Rm 6:10; Heb 7:27; cf. Jn 13:1; 17:1]. His Paschal mystery is a real event that occurred in our history, but it is unique: all other historical events happen once, and then they pass away, swallowed up in the past. The Paschal mystery of Christ, by contrast, cannot remain only in the past, because by his death he destroyed death, and

all that Christ is — all that he did and suffered for all men — participates in the divine eternity, and so transcends all times while being made present in them all. The event of the Cross and Resurrection abides and draws everything toward life.

Jesus both sacrificed himself and at the same time was murdered against his will as a victim of injustice through his physical sufferings and death on the cross. He did not commit suicide nor did he plot his own death. These murderous events were inflicted upon him by his torturers who in effect symbolized and really represented every sin of all mankind. As St. Francis of Assisi puts it so well as cited in CCC 598:

> Nor did demons crucify him; it is you who have crucified him and crucify him still, when you delight in your vices and sins.

Jesus' physical and mental sufferings, combined with his cluster of virtues shining through his sufferings, by his divine love merited our salvation. His virtues on the cross were mercy, obedience, humility, and patience alongside of the virtue of religion whereby he manifested his complete submission to the Father in adoration while on the cross. Without understanding these faith facts of Jesus' action on the cross, we cannot really understand the role and life of the ministerial priest.

It is one thing to merit special graces for one's family, friends, even enemies by offering our physically and spiritually pleasurable and virtuous acts while in the state of grace; yet, it is something other to manifest one's virtues for the glory of God in the midst of suffering. In Catholic theology such deeds are called acts of satisfaction or reparation or penance. All of us, laity and clergy, can offer both joyful and sorrowful good deeds to our heavenly Father depending on our morally upright lifestyles and the various kinds of crosses we all carry from time to time, whether light or heavy. In that sense, all of us are called to be victims with Christ. We may have to be victims unwillingly when physical, mental, social, or emotional suffering come our way, but we have to somehow make these unwilling incidents fruitful by willfully accepting them when there are no human or medical solutions, and offer them to our heavenly Father as penance for our sins and the sins of the whole world. This aspect of our lives is the exercise of the common priesthood of the laity, but it also includes in a special way that of the priest or deacon who is configured in a special way to Jesus the saving servant of all.

The Sacrament of Orders in General

Beyond doubt, when he receives the sacrament of Orders, the deacon, priest or bishop receives a special configuration to Jesus Christ (CCC 1585):

> The grace of the Holy Spirit proper to this sacrament is configuration to Christ as Priest, Teacher and Pastor, of whom the ordained is made a minister.

Here "configuration to Christ as Priest" does not necessarily mean that the ordained person shares in all the powers of priesthood (in Latin *sacerdos*). This sharing is reserved for the rank of bishop, yet the priest shares in many of the bishop's powers as well. While all three degrees of Orders conform one to Christ who is a priest, still one rank, that of deacon, does not become a *sacerdos* as we shall see below. Number 1581 of the CCC teaches:

> This sacrament configures the recipient to Christ by a special grace of the Holy Spirit, so that he may serve as Christ's instrument for his Church. By ordination one is enabled to act as a representative of Christ, Head of the Church, in his triple office of priest, prophet and king.

Again, as we will see further, the deacon, unlike the priest and bishop, is neither configured to Christ as a *sacerdos* (*sacerdoce*), nor does he ever become a "pastor," strictly speaking (cf. CIC 521 § 1), even though he shares in Christ's pastoral office (as stated in CCC 1585) and can participate in many functions of governance within the Church as seen in the *Code of Canon Law* for the Latin Church. (His functions are more restricted in the Canons of the Eastern Church.[1]) However, the specific office of pastor is reserved to the bishop and presbyter (the name also given to someone who belongs to the rank of priest) both of whom exclusively possess the ministerial *sacerdos*.

Orders Are for Others

The *Catechism* first teaches us that the sacrament of Holy Orders, like Matrimony, is a sacrament directed to the salvation of others (1534). The sacraments of Holy Orders and Matrimony also contribute to the personal salvation of the minister or married person because the work they do is a contribution to others (Ibid.), and both sacraments confer a "particular mission in the Church" to "build up the People of God" (Ibid.). Both sacraments bring a special consecration, though for Orders it is permanent and for marriage "until death."[2] For there is no character given in the sacrament of Matrimony as there is in the sacrament of Holy Orders. As the *Catechism* explains:

> 1581. This sacrament [Holy Orders] configures the recipient to Christ by a special grace of the Holy Spirit, so that he may serve as Christ's instrument for his Church. By ordination one is enabled to act as a rep-

---

[1] See *Code of Canons of the Eastern Churches*. The deacon ordinarily cannot baptize but only in the case of necessity (677 § 2), nor can he witness a marriage but he can preach (610 and 614 § 4).

[2] This explains why the phrase "as it were" is used just before the word "consecrate" for those who receive the sacrament of Marriage (CCC 1535).

resentative of Christ, Head of the Church, in his triple office of priest, prophet, and king.

1582. As in the case of Baptism and Confirmation this share in Christ's office is granted once for all. The sacrament of Holy Orders, like the other two, confers an indelible spiritual character and cannot be repeated or conferred temporarily (cf. Council of Trent: DS 1767; LG 21, 28, 29; PO 2).

The Degrees within Orders

The sacrament of Holy Orders continues the mission of the apostles until the end of time by three distinct **degrees** (CCC 1566). It is not three sacraments. It is one sacrament with three degrees, grades or levels (the various ways of looking at the Latin word *gradus* from the Council of Trent): episcopate, presbyterate, and diaconate. What is the meaning of the word *degree* in this context? CCC 1549 suggests the following:

> Through the ordained ministry, **especially** that of bishops and priests, the presence of Christ as head of the Church is made visible in the midst of the community of believers.

Whereas, number 1596 says regarding the deacon:

> Deacons are ministers ordained for tasks of the Church; they do not receive the ministerial priesthood, but ordination confers on them important functions in the ministry of the word, divine worship, pastoral governance and the service of charity, tasks which they must carry out under the pastoral activity of their bishop.

Are Deacons Members of the Hierarchy?

If we look to the *Catechism*'s section concerning the dogma that the Church is apostolic (874-96), the deacons are part of the hierarchical Church since the principal references are to the bishops as the heads of particular churches with the assistance of priests (877, 886 & 893) and deacons (886 & 894). What this implies is that under the bishop and priests, the deacons have some share in the teaching, sanctifying and governing of the Christian faithful. And *Lumen Gentium* 28 & 29 clearly taught:

> Thus the divinely instituted ecclesiastical ministry is exercised in different degrees by those who even from ancient times have been called bishops, priests and deacons (cf. Council of Trent, session 23, De sacr. ordinis, cap. 2: Denz. 958 (1765), and can. 6: Denz. 966 (1776).

> At a lower level of the hierarchy is to be found deacons, who receive the imposition of hands "not unto priesthood but unto ministry." For, strengthened by sacramental grace they are dedicated to the people of God, together with the bishop and his body of priests, in the service of the liturgy, of the Gospel and of works of charity.

In the *Catechism*, therefore, what is stated in numbers 874-79 is the Church's answer to why the ecclesial ministry as such applies to all three degrees of Holy Orders. In CCC 875, clearly the preacher needs to speak with authority and grace by an empowerment of Christ by which the minister acts due to the character of Orders in the person of Christ the head (*in persona Christi capitis*). Number 876 states that all sacred ministers have a service whereby they must "become slaves of all." In CCC 877, bishops are seen to exercise their ministry in a college and the priests in a presbyterium. The deacon as such does not belong to either; however, numbers 878 and 879 show that the sacramental nature of the diaconal acts (administration, teaching, and the imparting of some sacraments and sacramentals) is a service that has a collegial and personal character "exercised in the name of Christ." The rest of the numbers on this subject deal mostly with the bishop who possesses the highest degree of Orders and is, in some way, the model for the other two.

Finally, in number 939, we see how the hierarchical structure of the Church relates to itself as three degrees and to the rest of the faithful:

> Helped by the priests, their co-workers, and by the deacons, the bishops have the duty of authentically teaching the faith, celebrating divine worship, above all the Eucharist, and guiding their Churches as true pastors. Their responsibility also includes concern for all the Churches, with and under the Pope.

It should be noted that the deacons are purposely not called *co-workers* since they do not share in the ministerial priesthood; they are "at a lower level of the hierarchy" (LG 29). Also, they do not form a separate collegium as do the bishops and the priests since they do not pertain to the rank of *sacerdos* with all its associated sacred powers. It is theirs to "help and serve" those who pertain to the rank of *sacerdos* (priesthood), namely the episcopate and the presbyterate. Still the deacons are incorporated into a separate *ordo* or order (CCC 1537) which is why the Church calls the seventh sacrament *Holy Orders* in the plural. Although they do not participate in Christ's sacerdotal ministry, we need to keep in mind that they have their own role to fulfill when the Church celebrates her liturgy (1140) by its common priesthood from Baptism (1141). And, we must keep in mind:

> 1142. "...the members do not all have the same function." Certain members are called by God, in and through the Church, to a special service of the community. These servants are chosen and consecrated by

the sacrament of Holy Orders, by which the Holy Spirit enables them to act in the person of Christ the head, for the service of all the members of the Church. The ordained minister is, as it were, an "icon" of Christ the priest.

Why Is the Word *Orders* Used to Describe This Sacrament?

Returning now to the question of Orders, we see that numbers 1537 and 1538 neatly summarize the Church's traditional teaching that it is an *order* or an established body of persons given by a sacramental act (called in this case an *ordination*) which is also a consecration (CCC 1537-1538) since it is a "setting apart and an investiture by Christ himself for his Church." This act confers a gift of the Holy Spirit on bishops, priests or deacons that can "only come from Christ through his Church." This gift of the Holy Spirit brings with it "sacred power."[3]

The next numbers 1539-1543, try to show how the sacrament of Orders is related to the "priesthood of the Old Covenant" as seen in the priesthood of Aaron, the service of the Levites and the institution of the seventy elders of the Old Testament (Nb 11:24-25). According to the consecratory prayer for the deacon, he is related to the "sons of Levi" as cited in CCC 1543.

With the coming of Jesus Christ, there is in him one unique priesthood fulfilling everything found in the Old Covenant (1544). But there are only two, not three or more participations in this unique priesthood. One share is found in the whole community of believers (1546), the other essentially distinct part is the "ministerial or hierarchical priesthood of bishops and priests" (1547). It is clear in the teaching of the Church that the deacon is not included to indicate that the priest and bishop are closer to each other than to the deacon. This is based upon the fact

---

[3] There seems to be a slight confusion here in the text of the *Catechism* because the footnote refers to the ministerial priesthood not to Orders as such (LG 10).

that the priests and bishops possess differing powers (e.g., to confect the Eucharist, confer the Sacrament of the Sick, forgive sins, confect the sacrament of marriage for the Eastern Church — priests and bishops — and to confect the sacrament of Holy Orders — bishops only), none of which the deacon possesses by the will of Christ. Thus in number 1120 of the CCC, we find the Church teaching that all three ranks but especially the latter two ranks of priest and bishop do the following:

> 1120. The ordained ministry [in my words, the three ranks] or *ministerial* priesthood [in my words, the second and third rank exclusively] is at the service of the baptismal priesthood (cf. LG 10 §2). The ordained priesthood guarantees that it really is Christ who acts in the sacraments through the Holy Spirit for the Church. The saving mission entrusted by the Father to his incarnate Son was committed to the apostles and through them to their successors: they receive the Spirit of Jesus to act in his name and in his person (cf. Jn 20:21-23; Lk 24:47; Mt 28:18-20). The ordained minister is the sacramental bond that ties the liturgical action to what the apostles said and did and, through them, to the words and actions of Christ, the source and foundation of the sacraments.

Truly the bishop is the successor, in the fullest sense of the word, of the apostles (cf. also CCC 1313), the priest less so, and the deacon the least so.

At the same time, the Church, however, cannot say that there is a substantial difference between the deacon and bishop/priest. Otherwise one would falsely conclude that Holy Orders is really three separate sacraments. On the other hand, and here is where part of the conceptual difficulty lies, the deacon does not participate in the ministerial priesthood of Christ, though at the same time he does participate *in his own rank* the diaconate or service of Christ (who is priest, prophet, and king) so that he functions in *persona Christi capitis* in certain instances but to a lesser degree. He still does a sacred ministry but a lesser kind.

Those who are appointed to nourish the Church by word and sacrament are called, strictly speaking, ministers of the Gospel and they possess Holy Orders. But the rank of ministerial priesthood is a quality flowing from the character of Orders whereby the minister represents Christ the head in confecting sacraments which no one else has the power to do.

Who Is the Ministerial Priest and What Does He Do?

Up to now, I have explained the Church's teaching on Holy Orders in general and some teachings concerning the deacon. Now we turn to the brunt of our study: the priesthood. We will not endeavor to expose the nature of the episcopate; but much of what was already analyzed will continue to be applied to the priesthood in particular, which, in turn, can easily be applied to the bishop who possesses the fullness of Orders.

> 1547. In what sense (is the ministerial priesthood essentially different from the common priesthood of the laity)? While the common priesthood of the faithful is exercised by the unfolding of baptismal grace — a life of faith, hope, and charity, a life according to the Spirit, — the ministerial priesthood is at the service of the common priesthood. It is directed at the unfolding of the baptismal grace of all Christians. The ministerial priesthood is a means by which Christ unceasingly builds up and leads his Church. For this reason it is transmitted by its own sacrament, the sacrament of Holy Orders.

This number of the *Catechism* clearly teaches that the ministerial priest is someone who is a leader of the faithful so that the baptismal graces of the Christian faithful are properly developed and unfolded. He does this first by his proper administration of the sacraments, and second, by his life as a priest, necessarily including his prayer life.

The Priest's Identity

What then specifically marks out the ordained priest in his resemblance to Christ? In the apostolic exhortation of Pope John Paul II, *Pastores Dabo Vobis* (hereafter PDV), the fruit of the Synod of Bishops in 1990, the Holy Father answers this question saying: "Indeed, the priest, by virtue of the consecration which he receives in the sacrament of Orders, is sent forth by the Father through the mediatorship of Jesus Christ, to whom he is *configured in special way as head and shepherd of his people*, in order to live and work by the power of the Holy Spirit in service of the Church for the salvation of the world" (12b).

As head of the Church, his body, Christ exercises authority over her. This authority, however, is not one of dominion, but one of service. This service "attains its fullest expression in his death on the cross." Therefore, Christ's headship is best understood by his total gift of self (21).

As shepherd of the Church, his flock, Christ exercises compassion toward her. This is shown in the way that Christ "gathers," "protects," and "nourishes" his sheep. But the Good Shepherd is also one who will "lay down his life for his sheep," and so this image too is best understood by Christ's total gift of self on the cross (22).

As both head and shepherd, Christ expresses the "pastoral charity"[4] which he has for the Church, and which is fulfilled in a "total gift of self." This phrase, in turn, is best explained by the spousal love of Christ the Bridegroom for his Bride the Church

---

[4]   In another part of PDV (24e), pastoral charity is called an *amoris officium* following the terminology of St. Augustine.

(22c). It is the image of Christ the Bridegroom, then, which explains the priest's configuration to Christ as Head and Shepherd of the Church. How these three images are interrelated forms the profound theology of priesthood found in PDV.

Christ as Bridegroom and Head

The concept of "headship" is related to that of authority, and so the priest, configured to Christ the Head, "is endowed with a 'spiritual power' which is a share in the authority with which Jesus Christ guides the Church through his Spirit" (21a). This authority and power, however, shuns every "presumption or desire of 'lording over'" others (21e) in favor of a "service" which is a "humble and loving dedication [of self] on behalf of the Church" (21c). It is only in this way that Christ the Head exercises any authority. So too the headship of the priest is one of complete service.

To explain how Christ the Head also relates to the Church as Bridegroom, it is necessary to see how the Church herself can be both Christ's Body (related to Christ as Head) and his Bride (related to Christ as Bridegroom). To explain it, the Holy Father uses patristic imagery: just as Eve was taken from the body of Adam to become his bride, so the Church is "the bride who proceeds like a new Eve from the open side of the Redeemer on the cross" (22c). Thus she is both Christ's Body and his Bride, and when Christ relates to her as her Head, he must do so with the love of the Bridegroom.

Christ the Head's authority of service, then, completely coincides with Christ the Bridegroom's spousal love for the Church. Insofar as the priest is configured to Christ, his authority and love must coincide in the same way.

Christ as Bridegroom and Shepherd

It is easier for us to understand how Christ relates to the Church as both Bridegroom and Shepherd, i.e., how the compassion of the Good Shepherd is related to the spousal love of the Bridegroom. This compound imagery takes an interesting turn, however, as it is applied to the life of the priest. There, the Holy Father shows how the priest's spousal love for the Church is directly connected to his love for Christ himself, that is to say, how the priest's love for the Bride is dependent upon his love for the Bridegroom. The Holy Father recalls the Gospel text in which Jesus specifically commissions Peter: he "entrusted to Peter the ministry of shepherding the flock only after his three-fold affirmation of love [for Jesus]." It was only in consequence of Peter's affirmative answer to the question, "Do you love me?" that Jesus then said, "Feed my lambs. Feed my sheep." The Holy Father writes:

> The primary point of reference of the priest's charity is Jesus Christ himself. Only in loving and serving Christ... will charity become a source, criterion, measure and impetus for the priest's love and service to the Church (PDV 23e).

Therefore, the source of the priest's pastoral charity and spousal love for the Church must be and will only be found in his love for Christ.

This is not to denigrate the importance of the priest's sacramental configuration to Christ, which the Holy Father expresses in this way:

> The priest is called to be the living image of Jesus Christ, the spouse of the Church.... In virtue of his configuration to Christ, the head and shepherd, the priest stands in this spousal relationship with regard to the community. Inasmuch as he represents Christ,

the head, shepherd and spouse of the Church... [the priest] is called to live out Christ's spousal love toward the Church, his bride. Therefore, the priest's life ought to radiate this spousal character, which demands that he be a witness to Christ's spousal love (PDV 22d).

While it continues to be true, then, that the priest must be an *alter Christus*, in virtue of his sacramental configuration, the Holy Father gives equal play to the concept of the priest as an *amator Christi*, professing his love for Christ in order to receive his mandate as shepherd.

The priest's full bonding to Christ, then, is both ontological and existential. It is ontological, i.e., involving his very essence as a human being, as it derives from his sacramental configuration to Christ. But this essential bond must be put into action to give it life. And so the priest must also daily fan the flames of that bond to Christ through affective (prayer) and effective (doing his will) love.

From this intricate bond flows a whole host of responsibilities which define the priest's inner life (e.g., study and prayer) and his outer life of ministry (25a, 711 & 72h). Together, his inner and outer life, authentically and harmoniously lived, make up the priest's identity since "an intimate bond exists between the priest's spiritual life and the exercise of his ministry" (24c). And if he is a religious priest, his vows add a further modality to his life. As the old scholastic adage put it: *actio sequitur esse* or action follows a person's being.

Priestly Virtue and Character

Now given such a vision of what the essence of the priesthood is, what kind of mentality, attitudes and virtues are needed to live out the implications of that extraordinary bond? First, the priest must develop the spousal character of Christ the Bridegroom since he is called to live out Christ's love for the Church, his bride. Therefore, the priest's life ought to radiate this character. This demands that he be capable of loving people with a heart which is new, generous and pure — with genuine self-detachment, with full, constant and faithful dedication and at the same time with a kind of "divine jealousy" (cf. 2 Cor 11:2) — and even with a kind of maternal tenderness, capable of bearing "the pangs of birth" until "Christ be formed" in the faithful (cf. Gal 4:19, PDV 22d).

The Holy Father shows the intimate connection between Christ's spousal love for the Church — and the priest's — with the Eucharist which is the "center and root of the whole priestly life" (23f). It is in the Eucharist, he writes, that pastoral charity "has its full expression and its supreme nourishment" (23f). This is because the Eucharist "represents, makes once again present, the sacrifice of the cross, the full gift of Christ to the Church... the supreme witness of the fact that he is head and shepherd, servant and spouse of the Church" (23f).

Next, the priest must develop the virtues of leadership. As Christ is Head of his Body the Church, so too the priest must have all that is necessary to exercise spiritual leadership: "faithfulness, integrity, consistency, wisdom, a welcoming spirit, friendliness, goodness of heart, decisive firmness in essentials, freedom from overly subjective viewpoints, personal disinterestedness, patience, an enthusiasm for daily tasks, confidence in the value of the hidden workings of grace as manifested in the simple and the poor" (cf. Tt 1:7-8, PDV 27f).

Finally, the priest must develop the heart of Christ the Shepherd, going after the lost sheep of his flock. The effectiveness of this aspect of the priest's ministry will, in part, flow from his spirituality (25d). Since he is called to teach and preach the word of God, he must develop a prayerful sensitivity to the scriptures, tradition and the magisterium (the official teaching of the Church) (26b). Moreover, dispensing the sacraments and praying the liturgy of the hours, the priest discovers the deep unity between ministry and his spiritual life (26c).

As a supplement to the above, every priest needs what theology calls "counsels of ease": obedience, chastity, and poverty. Even when these are not professed as vows, as virtues they help him live up to the personal dignity and mission of one so profoundly joined to Christ:

> Jesus Christ, who brought his pastoral charity to perfection on the cross with a complete exterior and interior emptying of self, is both the model and source of the virtues of obedience, chastity and poverty which the priest is called to live out as an expression of his pastoral charity for his brothers and sisters (PDV 30g).

In PDV the Holy Father describes the virtue of obedience as apostolic, communitarian, and pastoral. It is "apostolic" in that it "recognizes, loves and serves the Church in her hierarchical structure" (28b). This involves a real "submission" to those whose authority ultimately derives from the apostles. Therefore the priest must form certain attitudes of humble submission to higher authority, e.g., to his bishop and Peter's successor (28b), just as he asks other people to obey his word.

The communitarian aspect of obedience recognizes the collaborative nature of the priest's mission: to be effective, he must be in solidarity with the full presbyterate. And this means a solidarity with all priests, including religious priests, who

> represent a spiritual enrichment of the entire diocesan presbyterate, to which they contribute specific charisms and special ministries, stimulating the particular church by their presence to be more intensely open to the Church throughout the world (PDV 31d).

This communitarian dimension of priestly obedience

> demands a marked spirit of asceticism, both in the sense of a tendency not to become too bound up in

> one's own preferences or points of view and in the
> sense of giving brother priests the opportunity to make
> good use of their talents and abilities, setting aside all
> forms of jealousy, envy and rivalry. Priestly obedience
> should be one of solidarity, based on belonging to a
> single presbyterate (PDV 28c).

Within this full presbyterate, obedience is expressed in co-re-
sponsibility regarding directions to be taken and choices to be
made (28e). Likewise, obedience is also pastoral. This simply
means that the priest must be, in a sense, "obedient" to the needs
and demands of the people entrusted to him.

The counsel of chastity — as manifested in the law of celibacy before ordination — is reaffirmed for the priests of both
the Latin Church and some Eastern Churches as well. It is a sign
of communion with Jesus Christ in his gift of self to the Church
(29a):

> The Church as the spouse of Jesus Christ, wishes to
> be loved by the priest in the total and exclusive man-
> ner in which Jesus Christ her head and spouse loved
> her. Priestly celibacy, then, is the gift of self *in* and *with*
> Christ *to* his Church and expresses the priest's service
> to the Church in and with the Lord (PDV 29d).

This gift and grace of God are available to those who ask for it
and continue to request it (29f). Thus the Holy Father can de-
clare that the order of presbyterate should be conferred "only
on men who have given proof that they have been called by God
to the gift of chastity in absolute and perpetual celibacy" (29b).

As with chastity, so poverty is based upon the fact that God
is the one supreme good and treasure who can fulfill and satisfy
his people more than any created good. Poverty indicates a freedom from undue attachment to material things and a responsible use of them (30a). In addition, poverty assures the priest

that he is not using the Church for his own needs. It also opens his heart to the poor and keeps him ready to sacrifice his own comforts for the sake of those whom Jesus sends him to serve (30c).

If, as PDV so strongly advises, these counsels of obedience, chastity, and poverty are essential to the character of every priest, so much more are they essential to the character of those priests who are also consecrated religious. Far from being any sort of mark of an imaginary hierarchical difference between diocesan and religious priests, these counsels are points of unity.

As PDV makes clear, these counsels are meant to be associated with the virtues which bind the priest to Christ as Head, Shepherd, and Spouse. What this means, then, is that priestly formation must be understood to be, most fundamentally and essentially, to form the seminarian in accordance with this lofty call.

The Priest and His Lifestyle

Being a creature of Adam and Eve, the priest has his own weaknesses to struggle against and crosses to bear even though he is joined to Christ in a special way. As the *Catechism* puts it:

> 1550. This presence of Christ in the minister is not to be understood as if the latter were preserved from all human weaknesses, the spirit of domination, error, even sin. The power of the Holy Spirit does not guarantee all acts of ministers in the same way. While this guarantee extends to the sacraments, so that even the minister's sin cannot impede the fruit of grace, in many other acts the minister leaves human traces that are not always signs of fidelity to the Gospel and consequently can harm the apostolic fruitfulness of the Church.

He is called to a life of holiness because of his profound link with the risen Lord who was full of merciful love, which he must try to reflect in all of his sacred ministry. By far the greatest segment of his life and his ministry is found in the celebration of the Eucharist:

> 1566. "It is in the Eucharistic cult or in the Eucharistic assembly of the faithful (synaxis) that they exercise in a supreme degree their sacred office; there, acting in the person of Christ and proclaiming his mystery, they unite the votive offerings of the faithful to the sacrifice of Christ their head, and in the sacrifice of the Mass they make present again and apply, until the coming of the Lord, the unique sacrifice of the New Testament, that namely of Christ offering himself once for all a spotless victim to the Father" [LG 28; cf. 1 Cor 11:26]. From this unique sacrifice their whole priestly ministry draws its strength [Cf. PO 2].

Therefore, it is essential that priests develop the art and science of prayer for the sake of the kingdom. As Pope John Paul II has said concerning priests:

> He must be a man imbued with the spirit of prayer. The more he is involved in his ministerial commitments, the more he must cultivate contemplation and inner peace, well aware that the heart of every apostolate consists in living union with God. Strong tenacious and faithful love for Jesus Christ: transparent and joyful observance of discipline, the care of worship, readiness to serve and communion with the hierarchy. All these previously mentioned virtues are transformed in him into a missionary spirit, a leaven of growth for the Church herself, a striving for true

catholicity and a guarantee of authentic evangelization.[5]

St. Thomas Aquinas teaches us that contemplation is not
only open to anyone (ST II-II 179, 1) but "it behooves every
Christian who is in the state of salvation to have some share in
contemplation" (*In III Sent.* D. 36, q. 1, a. 3, ad 5). The contemplative and apostolic way of life of the priest belongs especially to the celibate lifestyle. Human life itself (not just religious
life) is correctly divided into action and contemplation. We have
both sides to our personality, even if one predominates over the
other (ST II-II 179, 2 ad 2).

Spirituality as Underpinning the Lifestyle of the Priest

Spiritual progress or the way of perfection is always the way
of the cross since there is no holiness without some kind of self-
denial, struggle, asceticism, and mortification, all of which should
lead to the peace and joy of the Beatitudes (CCC 2015). If the
priest is supposed to be a man of contemplation, then these
words of the *Catechism* are similarly meant for him also. God
invites all to prayer no matter how far anyone runs from him or
hides from him (CCC 2567). The attentiveness of the heart of
Abraham, a man of silence whose decisions were made according to God's will, is essential to prayer (CCC 2570). Prayer re-
stores us to God's likeness and enables us to share in the power
of his life that saves the multitude (CCC 2572). Looking at the
wrestling of Jacob, the Church's spiritual tradition sees him as
an image of prayer as a struggle of faith and triumph of perseverance (CCC 2573). The prayer of Moses is characteristic of
contemplative prayer by which he remained faithful to his mission (CCC 2576). Similarly David and Elijah give their people

---

[5] "The heart of the apostolate lies in living union with God," *Osservatore Romano*,
June 9, 1993, p. 4, §5c.

an education in prayer (CCC 2578-81), not of flight from but rather an attentiveness to God's word (CCC 2584). Finally the Psalms ("The Praises") which form part of the prayer life of the priest show the meaning of a preferential love of the Lord that is still vulnerable to enemies and temptations, yet filled with hope in God's faithfulness, certain of his love and obedient to his will (CCC 2589). And as the priest achieves some modest growth in prayer he will come to realize what the *Catechism* teaches so beautifully:

> 221. But St. John goes even farther when he affirms that "God is love" (1 Jn 4:8, 16): God's very being is love. By sending his only Son and the Spirit of love in the fullness of life, God has revealed to us his most intimate secret (cf. 1 Cor 2:7-16; Eph 3:9-12.) God *is an eternal exchange of love, Father, Son and Holy Spirit, and destined us to share in that exchange* (emphasis mine).

And we are back to the haunting theme: the mystery of the priest as bridegroom lived out on the individual level. As he grows in the contemplative segment of his life, he develops an essential interiority. As he relates to his fellow priests in the presbyterate, and the parish where he may be involved as well (the active life), he manifests a certain exteriority or a mirror of his contemplative life. His future and lifelong challenge then is to join both the active and contemplative (ministry and communion) into a harmonious fruitfulness.

There is an invocation (CCC 1587) that the bishop of the Byzantine Rite prays over the priest at his ordination, which fittingly concludes this reflection on the inner being and life of the priest:

> Lord, fill with the gift of the Holy Spirit him whom you have deigned to raise to the rank of the priest-

hood, that he may be worthy to stand without reproach before your altar to proclaim the Gospel of your kingdom, to fulfill the ministry of your word of truth, to offer you spiritual gifts and sacrifices, to renew your people by the bath of rebirth; so that he may go out to meet our great God and Savior Jesus Christ, your only Son, on the day of his second coming, and may receive from your vast goodness the recompense for a faithful administration of his order.

Chapter Two

The Priest as Bridegroom and Spiritual Father

Part I

Our reflections begin with an old poem attributed to St. Norbert:

> O priest, who are you?
> Not through yourself, for you are drawn from nothing.
> Not for yourself since you are mediator of men.
> Not to yourself, for you are *married to the Church*.
> Not your own, for you are the servant of all.
> You are not you, for you are God. Who are you then?
> You are nothing and everything.[1]

Karl Hillenbrand has written the following concerning the relationship between the celibate priest and marriage:

> In *both cases* God is revealing himself: for this reason when I speak to young people who are thinking seriously about their choice I always stress the fact that a celibate priest should possess, after all, qualities similar to those required of a husband and father; however, he presents them in a different manner; sensitivity, a capacity for interpersonal relationships, and desire of cooperation, an openness to reconciliation....

---

[1] Cited by Cardinal Pierre Paul Philippe, OP, *The Virgin Mary and The Priesthood* (Staten Island, NY: Alba House), 1993, p. 24.

One should reflect on this in view of the emphasis in *Pastores Dabo Vobis* (n. 43) on the importance of the ability to form stable relationships and the need for a balanced cultivation of the emotions in those who are orientated toward priestly celibacy. This is essential also in light of a further consideration: the widespread *fear of relationships* is a sad feature of our era. It is not only potential candidates for the priesthood and religious life who wonder if they will be able to respect this choice of their whole life. The same fear is shared by young people who are concerned about living together as a couple and who, faced with alarming examples and statistics are skeptical about whether one can be faithful for life.[2]

An incomplete vision of what a ministerial priest is has settled around the idea of something he does as the mediator of Jesus Christ. Even Pope John Paul II recognized this problem of theological perspective when he noted on October 6, 1986: "We have not only received a mission, a function to be carried out in serving the people of God. Someone might speak of the priesthood as one would speak of a chore or of a function, all condensed to presiding over a Eucharistic gathering. But we do not live to be reduced just to be functionaries."[3]

The seminarian, according to *The Code of Canon Law* (248, 252 especially §3) is to be trained primarily with a speculative emphasis on moral and dogmatic theology and with a secondary emphasis on pastoral and communicative skills (by living some of his time out in a parish).[4] The idea of a spiritual year,

---

[2]   Fr. Karl Hillenbrand, "The priesthood and celibacy," *Osservatore Romano*, 31/32 (1302) 4-5 (4/11 August, 1993).

[3]   Cited in Philippe, *The Virgin Mary and the Priesthood*, p. 131.

[4]   Though the following observations are intended for diocesan priests, some concepts may apply now and again to monks, friars and other members of the consecrated life in so far as they are called to priestly existence.

quite new from the perspective of the Universal Church,[5] has been promoted for the purpose of grounding the seminarian in good habits of prayer. These underpin much of what he will become and do as presider at the liturgy and sacraments and as decision maker. His training must enable him to answer questions, preach, teach, and apply the Catholic faith to concrete situations, notwithstanding his many other roles of leadership.

One could begin reflecting on priestly formation from a little known sentence from the New Testament: "To you has been given a knowledge of the mysteries of the reign of God" (Mt 13:11). Part of a priest's function in the prophetic office of Christ is to articulate well on the verbal level. Moreover, his share in the kingly *munus* of Christ is to assume his role as an administrator, usually within a parish setting: arranging meetings, managing finances and perhaps overseeing a school and cemetery. Since he belongs to the college of presbyters, he must be able to feel at home and relate well with his fellow priests under the headship of his bishop. A priest needs to be capable of offering timely suggestions for the life of the diocese and to acquire the mind of his Ordinary, since he is his co-worker in the life of the diocese.

To achieve these functional goals, the seminarian needs to acquire habits of the heart and mind: study, prayer, self-discipline and dialogue. He could achieve these goals/habits (even holiness itself) whether married or not. In Latin Church law, he is called to a life of celibacy (or more descriptively, celibate pastoral charity/love), which he promises the ordaining prelate representing the Church during the rite of ordination to the transitional diaconate.[6] The homily suggested to the bishop in the ritual

---

[5] See *Pastores Dabo Vobis* of John Paul II, nn. 42, 62.

[6] Unlike the vowed religious, he does not make a vow of chastity but rather a promise of celibacy *for God*. He promises this because, in conjunction with his formators and spiritual directors, he recognizes that he has been given the charism of permanent celibacy as part of his graced life as a priest to be (cf. "Religious and the New Rite for the Ordination of Deacons," Francisco J. Egana, S.J., *Consecrated Life*, Vol. 17, No.2, 113-114). In a qualified sense, this promise made by a vowed religious is a distinct and further consecration of his life, flowing from his acceptance of the "clerical state" by ordination to the transitional diaconate (ibid., 113).

of ordination (1973), by speaking of the functionality of the deacon, clearly shows that celibacy is meant to be a "sign and stimulus of pastoral charity, a particular source of apostolic fecundity, a special form of consecration and of adherence with 'undivided heart' to Christ, which helps to serve more freely the work of supreme generation."[7]

Obviously the foregoing model of priesthood suggests something deep and far transcending any ordinary good which can be accomplished such as obtaining a doctorate in theology or canon law. To be filled with the perfections generated by a celibate lifestyle, the priest will only slowly incarnate each day of his life its significance; he will never really complete the task of being all that a priest should be until he enters heaven itself. The goal presented to him is open-ended, and like truth and beauty, as in any work of science or art, is never fully realized.

The Priest as Bridegroom

It came as a surprise to some when in 1976 the Sacred Congregation for the Doctrine of the Faith put out a document, *Inter Insigniores*, explaining in some detail why women cannot be ordained to the ministerial priesthood.[8] One argument that was offered ("iconic" in retrospect) was based upon symbolism, that is, the problem women would have imaging Christ the bridegroom.[9] Symbols not only appeal to the mind but grip the whole person in his senses and emotions. Hence, the importance theologically of tampering with them:

---

[7] *De institutione Lectorum et Acholythorum, De admissione inter candidatos ad Diaconatum et Presbyterum. De sacro caelibatu ampectendo*, Typis Polyglottis Vaticanis, 1972, ad 4. This articulates in liturgical law what Paul VI said in his encyclical letter of 1967 *Sacerdotalis celibatus*, §24-30.

[8] *Declaration on the Admission of Women to the Ministerial Priesthood* (*Inter Insigniores*), *Vatican Council II: More Postconciliar Documents* ed. by Austin Flannery, O.P., (Collegeville, MN: The Liturgical Press, 1982), pp. 428-40.

[9] Ibid. §5 ; see also the idea of priest as image of Christ in St. Thomas Aquinas, ST III 83, 1 ad 3.

It is through this scriptural language, all interwoven with symbols, and which expresses and affects man and woman in their profound identity, that there is revealed to us the mystery of God and Christ, a mystery which of itself is unfathomable... therefore, unless one is to disregard the importance of this symbolism for the economy of Revelation, it must be admitted that, in actions which demand the character of ordination and in which Christ himself, the author of the Covenant, the Bridegroom and Head of the Church, is represented, exercising his ministry of salvation — which is in the highest degree the case of the Eucharist — his role (this is the original sense of the word *persona*) must be taken by a man.[10]

Much later, John Paul II's Apostolic Letter *Mulieris Dignitatem* advances this same nuptial theme when it discusses the Paschal Mystery and the Eucharist. Christ's sincere gift of himself for his Bride in the Sacrifice of the Cross gives

...definitive prominence to the spousal meaning of God's love. As the Redeemer of the world, Christ is the Bridegroom of the Church. The Eucharist is the Sacrament of our Redemption. It is the Sacrament of the Bridegroom and the Bride.... It is the Eucharist above all that expresses the redemptive act of Christ the Bridegroom toward the Church the Bride. This is clear and unambiguous when the sacramental ministry of the Eucharist, in which the priest acts "in persona Christi," is performed by a man.[11]

---

[10] *Inter Insigniores*, p. 111 in *Acta Apostolicae Sedis*.

[11] *Mulieris Dignitatem*, n. 26. It has been argued that the nuptial dimension establishes the distinctive element of the priesthood of the New Covenant. See Gustave Martelet, S.J., "The Mystery of the Covenant and its Connections with the Nature of the Ministerial Priesthood," *Osservatore Romano*, English Edition, March 17, 1977, 6-7. See also St. Thomas Aquinas, ST III 82, 1 where he uses the phrase "in persona Christi."

Thus, the link between the nuptial mystery, the Eucharist, and the priesthood, found early in the Church's tradition has been reiterated in recent times.

When Bishop Blom of the diocese of San Diego, during the Roman Synod of 1991, also spoke of the priest as one "...ordained to represent and act *in persona Christi capitis ecclesiae*, to which I would add, *et sponsa Christi*,"[12] it may have seemed foreign to some clergy and many of the laity but it is not strange to the teaching Church.[13] I will explore this single image in this reflection, while keeping in mind that there are other metaphors and real analogies to help us understand the dignity and meaning of the priesthood. A seminarian may only vaguely understand this image since he is not yet a bridegroom; but eventually, if a seminarian perseveres in his ministry to his bride the Church as a priest, he will come to understand its implications more fully.

The custom of calling all ministerial priests "Father" here in the United States (a title accorded to religious priests only from the eighteenth century by the laity especially of France, Italy and Spain) contains the kernel of the idea of bridegroom. One can be a biological father alone, or spiritual father alone, or both (as is the case of the sacrament of marriage). The fatherhood of the priest is expressed very well in the *Decree on the Ministry and Life of Priests*, #16, by a biblical and patristic notion concerning the priest as a father in his role of finding a husband for his daughters:

---

[12] Bishop R. Blom, *Origins* 20 (1990) 307. He continues, "Through the imposition of hands and the outpouring of the Holy Spirit, priests are assimilated and configured to Christ, bridegroom of the Church, to be hers in love after the manner of Jesus in the pattern of his paschal activity. Here we have a spousal imagery the essence of the priesthood, to which are related both priestly ministry or function and priestly life."

[13] It certainly was clear in the ritual for bishops that they became bridegrooms of their diocese since this was the principle reason for the wearing of the ring as a sign of their marriage to a particular diocese (real in the case of ordinaries of the Latin rite, titular in the case of auxiliaries and others) but this is not explicitly mentioned in the Rite for Priesthood.

By means of celibacy, then, priests profess before men their willingness to be dedicated with undivided loyalty to the task entrusted to them, namely that of **espousing** the faithful to one husband and presenting them as a chaste virgin to Christ (cf. 2 Cor 11:2). They recall that mystical marriage, established by God and destined to be fully revealed in the future by which the Church holds Christ as her only spouse. Moreover they are made a living sign of that world to come, already present through faith and charity, a world in which the children of the resurrection shall neither be married nor take wives.

Yahweh and Christ as Bridegroom in the Sacred Scriptures

While it would be necessary to cite the entire Bible to show the theme of Yahweh as bridegroom, suffice it to mention Isaiah, 62:5 where the author says, "As the bridegroom rejoices over his bride, so shall your God rejoice over you"; or, "Since you became honorable in my eyes, you are glorious: I have loved you" (Is 43:4); or, "I will take you to myself for my people. I will be your God" (Ex 6:7). In the New Testament, it is a theme found in Mt 22:1-14, and the Book of Revelation or the Apocalypse 21:2, 9-10. All of these passages speak of God's desire to have the greatest possible love relationship with all of us.

Bridegroom in the *Catechism of the Catholic Church*

Turning now to the latest document to deal with the theme of Christ as the bridegroom of his Church, the *Catechism of the Catholic Church* (hereafter CCC) summarizes the "iconic" teaching in the following way:

796. The unity of Christ and the Church, the head and members of one body, also implies that the two are distinct but within a personal relationship often expressed by the image of bridegroom and bride. The prophets led up to the theme of the Messiah and his bride and John the Baptist proclaimed it (Jn 3:29). Jesus called himself the bridegroom; St. Paul spoke of the whole Church and of each of its faithful members as a bride pledged to Christ to become one spirit with him (Cf. Mt 22:1-14, 25:1-13; 1 Cor 6:15-17; 2 Cor 11:2). The Church is the spotless bride of the spotless lamb (Cf. Rev 22:17; Eph 1:4, 5:27). Christ loved his bride and "gave himself up for her, in order to make her holy" (Eph 5:25-26). He associates her with himself in an eternal covenant, and continues to care for her as for his own body (Cf. Eph 5:29).

This is the whole Christ, head and body, one formed from many... whether the head or members speak, it is Christ who speaks. He speaks in his role as head (*ex persona capitis*) and in his role as body (*ex persona corporis*). What does this mean? St. Paul says: "The two will become one flesh. This is a great mystery, and I am applying it to Christ and the Church" (Eph 5:31-32). And the Lord himself says in the Gospel: "So they are no longer two but one flesh" (Mt 19:6). So that you may know that these are in a sense two persons, and yet one in the union of marriage... *as head, he calls himself the bridegroom, as body, the bride* (St. Augustine, *En in Ps.*, 74.4: PL 36:948-949).

Consequences for the Ministerial Priesthood

Now, if the presbyter is a representation of Christ as priest, prophet, and king and acts *in persona Christi capitis*,[14] does it not follow as a further penetration into the mystery of Holy Orders that his sacramental consecration enables him likewise, according to the Roman document, *Inter Insigniores*, to share in Christ's own spousal relationship with the Church? The priest acts *in persona Christi* not only when he celebrates the sacraments, but also when he works to preach, teach and sanctify the people, and whether he is ill or retired. Even if the priest is imprisoned in solitary confinement, he sanctifies the Church by his suffering and prayer. He is permanently and constantly bound to the Church as the representation of her Head since he has been given a character which goes to the root of his being, and should therefore permeate everything he is and does, except for sin.

The Personal and Affective Love of the Priest for His People

The complete vision of *sacerdos* in the Latin Rite has profound ramifications for the seminary training programs as requested by *Pastores Dabo Vobis* of John Paul II. These still need to be enacted. To be a ministerial bridegroom of the Church (symbolized by the ring on a bishop's finger) implies something far more than being a mere professional functionary who provides sacraments like a circuit rider.[15] If humankind itself has been created with a constant attraction to a "beyondness," a yearning for a gift from the infinite and transcending God, then the priest has to lead each person to that goal. How is he going to do such a thing?

---

[14] *The Catechism of the Catholic Church*, #1548 quoting LG 10; 28; SC 33; CD 11; PO 2; 6; 13.

[15] Or, from another point of view, as put so humorously by Monsignor Thomas Kennedy of the Archdiocese of San Francisco: "The pastor takes care of leaks, lights, locks, litter, little league and does a little liturgy."

A married man dreams, thinks, imagines, feels, and wills deeply concerning his wife and children — all things which a husband does naturally by recollection and reminiscence. So too must something like this be done by the priest. By his affective love a husband nourishes and fosters acts of affirmation in his wife and children who in turn sense his love of them and wish to respond accordingly. It is not enough for him to "effectively" love them in terms of being a provider for their material needs, but rather he must also provide for their spiritual needs by an affective love. This means he must learn to cultivate a permanent, faithful, and exclusive bond or attachment to his wife, and to some extent his children (who will leave the nest someday). Such attachment to his wife, deepened by sexual intercourse and other acts of intimacy, will nourish his dedication and inflame his devotion to her and through her to their children by manifesting his effective friendship through communication, sacrifice, and the spirit of flexibility in leading the family. As Germain Grisez has written so well:

> One advantage of marriage as a vocational commitment by comparison with, say, the priesthood is that its duties generally concern others — spouse and children — to whom one is emotionally attached. That makes it somewhat easier to make the sacrifices required to live up to the commitment than if one's duties pertain to people with whom one has weaker emotional bonds.[16]

Equality and Diversity

The teaching of the Church is quite clear on the question of the sexes. They are equal in dignity, but complementary in

---

[16] Germain Grisez and Russell Shaw, *Fulfillment in Christ: A Summary of Christian Moral Principles* (Notre Dame, IN: University of Notre Dame Press, 1991), p. 333.

their corresponding differences.[17] Men and women can generate children but only the woman can nurture them in her womb and feed them from her breasts. Only men can be fathers, only women can be mothers. While women are to be obedient to their husbands, this is not a call for men to dominate their wives.[18] Obedience does not negate the important notion that husbands must be subordinate to their wives to the point of being willing to even die for them. The CCC confirms this view of St. Paul.[19] Marriage means partnership (spouse meaning "helper") and friendship, each contributing generously to the common good of the family and taking over the other's roles when sickness or other circumstances require this according to the talents of each.

Now, what should happen on the level of human marriage (but often, unfortunately, does not), must in some higher way be accomplished by the priest. The ministerial priest of the Latin Rite is meant to be a married man analogously, not in the carnal sense, but in a profoundly spiritual sense (which should also affect his emotions). The priest finds his identity in part by reflecting on the Trinity itself. In the very heart of God is found all the perfection of masculine and feminine, husband and wife, perfections found within the very unity of God, and in the very trinitarian relationships themselves. As the CCC says so beautifully:

> 221. But St. John goes even farther when he affirms that "God is love" (1 Jn 4:8, 16): God's very being is

---

[17] John XXIII, Allocution to the Federation of Young Catholic Women, in *The Pope Speaks*, 6 (1959-60), 331.

[18] "Again, and in this the conjugal union chiefly consists, let wives never forget that next to God they are to love their husbands, to esteem them above all others, yielding to them in all things not inconsistent with Christian piety, a willing and ready obedience." Taken from *The Catechism of the Council of Trent*, trans. Callen and McHugh (Rockford, IL: TAN Books, 1982), p. 352. See also, Pius XI, *Casti Connubi*, 26, 74; John XXIII, *Ad Petri Cathedram*, 53 where the popes consistently teach that the wife owes obedience to her husband.

[19] See *Catechism of the Catholic Church*, 1643 where each is called to be subject to one another. St. Thomas says the priest must be willing to die for his flock (ST II-II 40, 2).

love. By sending his only Son and the Spirit of love in the fullness of life, God has revealed to us his most intimate secret (cf. 1 Cor 2:7-16; Eph 3:9-12). *God is an eternal exchange of love, Father, Son and Holy Spirit, and he has destined us to share in that exchange* (emphasis mine).

This is not to say that the Trinity is to be understood as two "hims" and a "her." To the contrary, in line with sacred scripture and dogmatic definitions, the Blessed Trinity is a revealed analogy in three masculine terms, Father, Son and Holy Spirit. Holy Spirit in Greek and Hebrew would normally be translated in the feminine but all the manuscripts we have indicate that Jesus breaks the rules of grammar and always calls the Holy Spirit "He." While these relationships within God are not a marriage commonly understood, we can say that they are what marriage is supposed to be: an inter-relationship of community based upon a procession of truth and a spiration of self-giving love. Likewise, the persons of the Blessed Trinity remain distinct within their ineffable union. Moreover, since the Triune God has created humankind and redeemed it through Jesus Christ from the fall and its effects, the arrival of the Savior is spoken of in terms of marriage.

Sacerdotalis Caelibatus: Looking Back

Older priests recall from their formation that an attempt was often made to explain the promise of celibacy as a renunciation or severing of something for the sake of either a deeper relationship to Christ or more freedom to serve his Church. The emphasis was usually placed on what he must renounce: sexual intimacy with a member of the opposite sex, possessing children of his own and the family life that goes with it.

Pope Paul VI's encyclical letter, *Sacerdotalis Caelibatus* §56, speaks of this voluntary promise in the language of renunciation.

However, many ignored what was brought out and developed in the other fifty-five paragraphs in more positive language.

No one doubts that many priests from time to time feel the pains of a lack of intimacy in their lives, an inability to share their dreams and hopes, their sorrows and frustrations, joys and delights with a particular wife. Even *Sacerdotalis* §10 acknowledges that there are both lonely and bitterly discouraged priests.

Celibacy as a Vocation

The Church teaches that celibacy is both a gift and a challenge, being both a grace (a *donum* in the *Code of Canon Law*, 247, §1), a golden law (*Sac. Cael.* §3), a special spiritual gift, a badge and encouragement of charity, a special token of the rewards of heaven and a commitment requiring a certain affective and sexual maturity based on asceticism (*Sac. Cael.* §70, 77-78). CCC teaches that chastity itself is already a moral virtue and gift from God which must develop into self-giving, whether in marriage or celibacy for the kingdom (CCC 2337-2349, 1579). Love which is genuine is a total gift to the Lord and his Church (*Sac. Cael.* 78), *exclusive*, stable, a spur to all forms of heroism. Yet from experience, we know that priests can and do sin and have been unfaithful to their promise of celibacy. Why?

Much of the problem has stemmed from several converging sources: in the past, an under-valuation of marriage and family life as if it were not a vocation[20]; in the present, an over-valuation of the same realities as if the sacrament of marriage were

---

[20] One has only to look at the author Hans Urs von Balthasar to find the continuation of such pre-conciliar thinking. See his *The Christian State of Life*, trans. by Mary Frances McCarthy (San Francisco: Ignatius Press, 1989), p. 421.

the exclusive model of holiness and normality.[21] For the priestly candidates of the past, the problems may have included an undue emphasis on the ascetical means of growing in perfection of chastity as if they (the means) and chastity itself were ends in themselves. Finally, there has been a failure to understand the spousal/paternal role of the priest and the ignorance of the traditional teaching on contemplation without which **his spousal and paternal role cannot be fulfilled.**

For the priest, this means that while he renounces a one flesh union with a woman and offspring coming from that union, to be sure, he does not renounce the deepest meaning of marriage which is ultimately found both in God whom he represents and in the life of Jesus Christ whom he more directly imitates by acting *in persona Christi capitis*. Priestly celibacy needs to be understood through a precise analogy between Christ and the mystery of marriage not simply through a metaphor like that of shepherd. Thus, while our ordinary understanding of marriage is a one flesh union between a man and a woman in an exclusive relationship (Eph 5:25, 28-29, 32-33), this kind of bond does not exhaust the mystery of interpersonal relationship: that is, Christ's love of the Church is a kind of marriage of which the one flesh union is only a faint resemblance. Now this mystery and meaning of marriage belongs to the priest as it does to married couples, but the way it is lived is radically different and distinct. Both the priest and married couples live the mystery of an interrelationship or a mutuality of persons. Both generate children, one physical and spiritual and supernatural, the other purely spiritual and supernatural.

---

[21] Yet the religious state claims to anticipate heaven because there is no marriage in heaven. Also, it has been the ordinary teaching of the Church that virginity and celibacy for the "kingdom of heaven" complement the sacrament of marriage (*In IV Sent.*, D.38, q.1, a.5 and *Familiaris Consortio*, 16). It points to heavenly communion inclusive of all, surpassing the limitations of the most intimate communion men and women can experience on earth. But, see the new *Catechism* 1642, where it states clearly that marital love and family life gives to a couple a "foretaste of the Lamb's wedding feast."

Contemplation as the Key

So, the seminarian must learn to become *like* the young engaged man to his bride the Church, whether he is to be a Trappist monk in the wilderness somewhere, a scholarly Jesuit, or a parish priest to the poor or the rich. The way he does this substantially, but not exclusively, is to acquire the spirit and practice of contemplative prayer. Even the hermit's priesthood must in some way become a true *contemplata aliis tradere*, not in the direct sense of the pastoral ministry but in the spiritual communication of his prayer life to his bride living in the world (and out of the world in purgatory).

If the ministerial priesthood is a mystery of faith, then as the Church from the laity to the Pope contemplates this reality, she penetrates ever more deeply into its meaning. Hence each seminarian must discover the rich dimensions of contemplation (acquired and infused) so that his future priesthood may become both effective and holy.

The Journey through the Stages of Contemplation

The best way to help the seminarian grow into what he must become is through what many schools of spiritual theology call mental prayer. This is his greatest challenge: to be patient with the lack of results from his prayer. He lives in a very pragmatic and practical world and it wants immediate results. Hence he must try to learn the importance of the contemplative breadth of his present and future priestly life, which means waiting for the Lord's gifts. Otherwise, as experience proves over and over, his life will become compartmentalized, lacking basic general unity of life and force, each compartment tending to become the overarching concern of his life.

When the contemplative dimension of priesthood is treated either as an escape from his priestly responsibilities, or is simply neglected, then the highest law of the Church, the salvation of souls,[22] will become the occasion of burnout and corresponding discouragement. Consecrated celibacy, instead of being a source of life and spiritual fertility, will develop into an occasion of bitterness, and the priest will act the role either of a crabby bachelor or an overgrown adolescent constantly imposing his will upon his "bride," the parish or other ecclesial communities.

Contemplation in the Life of the Priest as Spouse

In one document of the Second Vatican Council, the Fathers described the Church as always "eager to act and yet devoted to contemplation" (SC 2). When it comes to infused contemplation, we have to agree with St. Teresa of Avila that contemplation is a gift which cannot be forced from God. However, we can and must prepare ourselves for the gift.[23] The reason why so few of us receive what should be normal accompaniments of growing in grace is that very many of us reject the day by day graces of the priestly life, and so, the heart is not prepared to receive the deeper favors of the Lord.

When the priest does not know how to contemplate through mental prayer, or even through the rosary (CIC 246 §3; 276 §1,5), he becomes a working functionary who loses the sense of his own mystery and the mystery of his bride the Church as well. If he becomes mixed up in feverish activity (work or ministry pursued for its own sake or out of compulsion), he quickly loses a relish for prayer, both liturgical and private. The words of Aquinas are fertile with suggestive spirituality for a busy priest:

> It is the function of the active life to ponder a truth interiorly so that we may be guided by it in external

---

[22] "...the salvation of souls, which is always the supreme law of the Church" (c. 1752 which happens to be the last line of the *Code of Canon Law*).

[23] Teresa of Avila, *The Mansions*, ed. by Marcelle Auclair (New York: Doubleday, 1961), p. 109.

actions; it is a function of the contemplative life to ponder on an intelligible truth interiorly and take delight in the consideration and love of it. Thus, Augustine says, *Let them choose for themselves the better part,* that is, the contemplative life, *let them dedicate themselves to the word, yearn for the sweetness of truth, occupy themselves with saving knowledge.* Thus he clearly states that teaching has its place in the contemplative life (ST II-II 181, 3).

Precisely so that he does not wear himself out in routine, the priest is called to spend time in meditation and mental prayer among his other spiritual obligations (CIC, 276 §5).

Nor is it by accident that the Church makes her own the mystical doctrines of St. Teresa of Avila and St. John of the Cross, even if they were trying to convey to their own Carmelites the meaning of their personal vocation as contemplatives. As we shall see, CCC teaches that contemplation is at the heart of all vocations, priestly or lay, single or married. But first, let us seek the wisdom of St. Thomas on this question.

Part II
St. Thomas and the *Catechism of the Catholic Church* on the Contemplative and Active Life

One could say that even though St. Thomas wrote for Dominican friars beginning in the science of theology, the Western Church in our time has taken over his doctrine as a model for all candidates to the clerical priesthood of the Latin Rite (CIC, 252 §3). The well-known teaching of Thomas, that contemplation should lead to handing on the fruits of contemplation to others in charity, is not meant to be something reserved to the Dominican Order. It is a model for all priesthood (ST II-II 188, 6). In the text (not directly cited), he makes a defense of his own Order, but it remains true for anyone that it is always normative to contemplate and give the fruits of this contemplation to others in charity (assuming this is God's will and the particular contemplative's vocation to the active ministry), precisely because charity/love is the highest law of the Christian.

For St. Thomas, contemplation is not only open to anyone (ST II-II 179, 1) but "It behooves every Christian who is in the state of salvation to have some share in contemplation" (*In III Sent.* D. 36, q. 1, a. 3, ad 5). The contemplative and apostolic way of life as a state belongs especially to the celibate. Some religious institutes are dedicated to contemplation in a primary way, others are more occupied with the works of the apostolate. However, human life itself (not just religious life) is correctly divided into action and contemplation. We have both sides to our personality, even if one or the other predominates (II-II 179, 2 ad 2).

Aquinas delineates several perspectives: the active life (of virtue) precedes contemplation in one way, as preparation for contemplation. It also directs the virtues as the higher reason provides the ultimate principles for lower reason to excogitate. Thomas uses an interesting analogy: as husband (contemplative side of the human person) directs the wife (active side of the human person). Of course he is not necessarily calling a male spiritually superior since many women are obviously more excellent contemplatives.

Aquinas makes the observation (ST I-II 38, 4; cf. II-II 180, 7) that the pleasure in contemplation is exceedingly delightful:

> We have seen that the contemplation of truth is the greatest of all pleasures (3, 5). We have seen too that every pleasure assuages pain. The contemplation of truth therefore assuages pain; and it does so the more perfectly one loves wisdom. This is why men find joy in the midst of tribulation by contemplating the things of God and the happiness to come; as the epistle of James says, *Consider yourselves happy indeed, my brethren, when you encounter trials of every sort.* What is

more, this joy occurs even in the midst of bodily tor-
ture; thus the martyr Tiburtius walking barefoot on
burning coals said, *I feel that I am walking on roses, in
the name of Jesus Christ.*

The function of contemplating and the object contemplated
blend in the act of contemplation, since contemplation is a kind
loving knowledge or a knowing shot through with love. Then,
when God is the end of contemplation, this delight surpasses
every delight. As one grows in this spiritual delight, it becomes
greater than carnal pleasure, and acts in turn as a stimulant for
growth in the virtue of chastity. St. Thomas warns us that no
human person can exist without delight and when he cannot
enjoy the delights of the spirit, he seeks those of the flesh (ST I-
II 35, 2 ad 2).

Chastity and Contemplation

In the beginning of the adolescent's journey for growth in
premarital chastity, there is much strife and struggle for self-
control or self-possession (cf. CCC 2342-43). This is necessary
for all those who are called to the married state so that they can
give themselves generously in persevering friendship exclusively
and permanently until death.[24] When someone is given a special vocation to priesthood or religious life, the struggle is similar but also different. Not only must he pray and strive for the
gift of permanent celibacy until his death (his spouse the Church
will never die), but he must endure and resist the tensions drawing him away from his personal growth in the contemplative dimension of his being.[25] To contemplate requires continuous ef-

---

[24] *Catechism* 2347 explicitly teaches that chastity is to blossom into friendship of
virtue (spiritual communion).
[25] The *Catechism* suggests such in 2731 (dryness in prayer), 2732 (lack of faith) and
2733 (acedia or depressing apathy).

fort to grow in two ways: sheer concentration of the intellect, and a determined will to be attentive to the primary object of contemplation, the awareness of God (CCC 2699) and understanding of the object of faith, namely the Triune God in himself, the Incarnation, and all things in relationship to him. Two major areas of potential growth are designated by the prayer side and the study side of a contemplative's personality, which at first seem opposites but are not really contradictory to one another. Emotions may deflect his attention from God and cause him to turn away from the activity of contemplating. However, St. John of the Cross said that when God is known by desire and understanding, carnal knowledge withers.[26] But getting to this point requires constant work to resist the siren songs of the world and flesh. As St. John of the Cross writes in *The Dark Night*:

> ... For when the friendship is purely spiritual, the love of God grows with it; and the more the soul remembers it, the more it remembers the love of God, and the greater the desire it has for God; so that, as one grows, the other grows also. For the spirit of God has this property, that it increases good by adding to it more good, since there is likeness and conformity between them. But when this love arises from the vice of aforementioned sensuality, it produces the contrary effects; for the more the one grows, the more the other decreases, and the remembrance of it similarly. If that sensual love grows, it will at once be observed that the soul's love of God is becoming colder, and that it is forgetting Him as it remembers that love; there comes to it, too, a certain remorse of conscience. And on the other hand if the love of God grows in the soul, that other love becomes cold and is forgotten; for, as

---

[26] This is actually an old traditional idea stemming from St. Gregory the Great. See Aquinas's incorporation of the idea, ST II-II 180, 7.

the two are contrary to the other, not only does the one no longer aid the other, but the one which predominates **quenches and confounds the other and becomes strengthened in itself** (bk 1, ch. IV).[27]

Yet what about people who are impulsive? Are they not more suited to active life because their emotions are not yet attuned to the peacefulness of contemplation? Being restless, they find it hard to concentrate on objects that transcend the senses (the Triune God) but tend instead to concentrate on tasks. Yet they not only need but can develop the contemplative side of their personalities, though it takes time to discover and practice this secret. All priests must learn to contemplate, but not all can or should live a contemplative lifestyle, since most are called to the active ministry. As Pope John Paul II has said concerning priests:

> He must be a man imbued with the spirit of prayer. The more he is involved in his ministerial commitments, the more he must cultivate contemplation and inner peace, well aware that the heart of every apostolate consists in living union with God. Strong tenacious and faithful love for Jesus Christ: transparent and joyful observance of discipline, the care of worship, readiness to serve and communion with the hierarchy. All these previously mentioned virtues are transformed in him into a missionary spirit, a leaven of growth for the Church herself, a striving for true catholicity and a guarantee of authentic evangelization.[28]

---

[27] *The Collected Works of St. John of the Cross*, trans. by Kieran Kavanaugh and Otilio Rodriguez (Washington, DC: ICS Publications, 1964), p. 341.

[28] "The heart of the apostolate lies in living union with God," *Osservatore Romano*, June 9, 1993, p. 4, §5c.

Celibacy for the kingdom, when lived in the spirit of contemplation, is not a great sacrifice but a great reward, a great delight as one grows in the virtues which prepare for and sustain it. As St. Thomas put it so masterfully:

> In both respects the **delight of contemplation surpasses every human delight. For spiritual delight is greater than carnal pleasure,** as we stated when discussing the passions, and because the love whereby God is loved out of charity surpasses all other love. Thus we read in Psalms, *Taste and see that the Lord is sweet* (ST II-II 180, 7).

> Although the contemplation of divine things is not full in this life, it is nevertheless greater than any other contemplation, however perfect, because of the excellence of that which is contemplated. Thus Aristotle says, *We may have our little theories about those most excellent beings and divine substance, and though we comprehend them only in part, nevertheless the mere honor of knowing them causes us more delight than all other things around us.* Gregory says the same thing, *The contemplative life is an exceedingly lovable sweetness which carries the soul above itself, reveals heavenly things and manifests spiritual realities to the mind's eye* (ibid., ad 3).

If we consider contemplation as a necessary aspect of friendship with God, the words of St. Thomas (ST I-II 38, 3) further indicate how it can overcome many difficulties in the active apostolate:

> It is natural in sorrow to be consoled if a friend shares our grief. Aristotle suggests two reasons.

> First, sorrow weighs one down; it is a load which, of course, one tries to lighten. When therefore a person sees others joining him in sorrow, it feels as if they

are helping him carry the load, trying to lessen its weight on him. So the burden weighs on him less heavy, just as in the case of carrying physical weight.

The second reason is a better one. When a person's friends share in his sorrow, he sees that they love him and this fact itself is a source of pleasure... (32, 5). But we have also seen that all pleasure assuages sorrow. It follows therefore that sorrow is assuaged by a friend's sharing it.

As matter of education and habit formation, this doctrine must be taught in seminaries as part of spiritual formation. Again as the Pope puts it:

The 1971 Synod of Bishops insisted particularly on "contemplation of the word of God" (footnote omitted). One should not be frightened by the word "contemplation" and the spiritual commitment it entails. It could be said that, independently of forms and lifestyles among those of the contemplative life, it nonetheless remains the most splendid jewel of Christ's Bride: the word of God in a contemplative spirit is valid for everyone, so that hearts and minds may be nourished on it. This helps the priest to develop a way of thinking and of looking at the world with wisdom, in the perspective of its supreme purpose: God and his plan of salvation. The Synod says: "To examine the events of life in the light of the Gospel" (footnote omitted).[29]

Hence the need exists for fixed periods of prayer and beautiful liturgy in the seminary and in one's priestly life.[30] What seems

---

[29] John Paul II, "Priests must be devoted to prayer," *Osservatore Romano*, June 9, 1993, p. 1, §4.

[30] See the *Catechism* 2709 on mental prayer and 2715-19 on contemplation. For liturgical music, see 1157, the icon 1159 and 1162.

(and is) a great sacrifice for beginners becomes an extreme delight of the spirit, which in turn leads to an energetic way of witnessing to the kingdom. From this perspective the celibate lifestyle is not negative but very positive. Aquinas in his treatment of the gift of Wisdom attests to this (ST II-II 45, 1-6).[31] The problem for priests is not celibacy seen as the absence of a spouse, but loneliness which can also exist in marriages!

The Absolute Necessity to Learn the Art of Acquired Contemplation

Raissa Maritain, the wife of Jacques, wrote eloquently concerning this art of contemplation:

> Contemplation is like a water-wheel which draws up the water and makes it flow into channels. If contemplation ceased entirely, hearts would soon be dried up (because all love presupposes a contemplation of the desired object).[32]

> Contemplative prayer is not a question of making God descend from heaven! He is already there in us by grace. It is a question of descending into ourselves, to the bottom of our soul, and that, once again, by sweeping away obstacles.[33]

> Where does Love die? The Friend replies that it is in the pleasures of this world. Where does love live and nourish itself? In meditating on the other world.[34]

---

[31] The *Catechism* attests and confirms the teaching on the existence of the seven gifts of the Holy Spirit in 1830-31.

[32] *Raïssa's Journal* presented by Jacques Maritain (Albany, NY: Magi Books, 1981) p. 73.

[33] Ibid., p. 75.

[34] Ibid., p. 174.

Now this activity is already the beginning of a spousal dynamic operating in the seminarian on the level of living. As one grows in his contemplative life, he is developing an interiority. As he relates to his fellows in community (the active life), he manifests a certain exteriority or a mirror of his contemplative life. **His future and lifelong challenge is to wed both the active and contemplative (ministry and communion) into a harmonious, fruitful relationship.** Aquinas teaches us (ST II-II 180, 3 ad 4) that any contemplative must receive doctrine from others through preaching, teaching and writing. Then he must pray over and meditate upon the divine mysteries he has learned (especially of the Trinity), meditation yielding to pondering and gazing over them, full of awe at their excellence. The contents of the faith about the thrice holy God are not mere ideas, but realities with which he is already in union by grace. Following St. Thomas' insight, we do not believe in formulas but in the realities they express (CCC 170).

And thus we return to the haunting theme: that is, the mystery of marriage lived out on the individual level. As the seminarian grows in his contemplative life, he is developing an essential interiority. As he relates to his fellows in community and the parish where he may be involved as well (the active life), he manifests a certain exteriority or a mirror of his contemplative life.

Spirituality in the *Catechism* as Underpinning the Lifestyle of the Seminary

Spiritual progress (something that all seminarians and most priests eagerly desire) means more intimate union with Christ, a union which is called mystical as far as it comes through the sacraments (sacred mysteries). The extraordinary signs or special graces of this mystical life that are given to a few saints and blesseds are meant to be signs that God's undeserving gift is given to all (CCC 2014). However, the way of perfection is always the way of the cross as there is no holiness without some kind of self-denial, struggle, asceticism and mortification (the life of the seminary whether traditional or modern) all of which should lead to the peace and joy of the Beatitudes (2015). If the future priest is supposed to be a man of contemplation, he must explain the following texts to his people. These are now part of the Magisterium of the Church. No one can say that contemplation is only reserved for contemplatives in view of the many reference texts in the new *Catechism* which will be cited below, as applied to the priest.

Kinds of Prayer in the *Catechism*

There are four kinds of prayers: blessing and adoration, petition, intercession, thanksgiving and praise, all of which are contained in the Eucharist (CCC 2643). Blessing God is the basic movement of Christian prayer (2626). In number 1078 of the *Catechism*, we learn that blessing God means worshiping and surrendering to our Creator in thanksgiving. Moreover, adoration is the first attitude of those who acknowledge themselves to be creatures before their Creator, an homage of the mind, respectful silence blended with humility and giving assurance to our prayers (2648). The vocabulary of supplication, richly diverse in the New Testament, is petition by which we express an awareness of our relationship with God. We are not our own beginning, nor masters of our fate, nor our own last end (2629). Since we are sinners, the first movement of petition is asking for forgiveness (2631). Further, petition is centered on the desire and quest for the coming of the kingdom. Intercession is the prayer of petition for all people in imitation of Jesus (2634). Every event and need can also become the occasion of an offering of thanksgiving (2638). Finally, praise is the recognition that God is God and it sings His glory, not for what He has done, but simply because He is what He is (2639).

The Scriptures are the surpassing way of knowing Jesus

(2653) "Seek in reading and you will find in meditating; knock in mental prayer and it will be opened to you by contemplation" (2654, citing Guigo the Carthusian). During the liturgy of the Church, prayer becomes interiorized and assimilates its spirit during and after its celebration (2655). It is also the atmosphere of the three theological virtues (2656-60).

Expressions of Prayer Under the Holy Spirit

Prayer is expressed in words, melodies, gestures and even iconography (CCC 2663). Our access to the Father is always through Christ (2665). The name Jesus (Yahweh saves) contains all: God, humanity and whole economy of creation and salvation (2666). The invocation of the holy name of Jesus is the simplest way of praying always. Repeated often by a humbly attentive heart, it bears much fruit with patient endurance and it is always a prayer that is possible for everyone, being the part of one's daily life: loving God which animates and transfigures every action in Christ Jesus (2668). In a certain sense, praying the name of Jesus contains the devotion to the Sacred Heart and the Way of the Cross since we are with Jesus in all his mysteries (2668-69). The Holy Spirit whose anointing permeates our whole being is the interior teacher and artisan of Christian prayer with its many paths (2672); so we can say Christian prayer becomes prayer in the Church (Ibid.).

By the Holy Spirit, we are united to the Person of the only Son and initiated into communion in the Church with Mary (2673). She is our mother who is altogether transparent to him, that is, she is the sign who shows us the way to him. All the churches developed their prayer to Mary centering it on the person of Christ manifested in his mysteries. Two movements alternate with each other to Mary, one magnifying the Lord, and the other, entrusting praises and supplication to Mary because the Church recognizes that in her is the humanity embraced by God's son (2875). Mary, figure of the Church, is the perfect "pray-er." When we pray to her, we hold with her to the plan of the Father for us. We can also pray with as well as to her (2678).

There are many spiritualities of prayer based upon liturgical and theological currents of the past and present (2684) which the seminarian and the priest is free to choose once he is exposed to them, following the inspirations of the Holy Spirit and his personal inclinations. While the family is the first place of prayer (2685), ordained ministers are also responsible for formation in prayer. Even persons in the consecrated life, when fervent, are living sources of contemplation and the spiritual life of the Church (2687) and every form of consecrated life can have its own associates or members of a Third Order (sometimes called by other names now, CIC 303). In catechesis or popular piety, memorization of prayers is essential while the meaning is understood (2688). Prayer groups today are a sign of renewal in prayer (2689) which anyone has the freedom to join. In number 2689, the use of spiritual directors who are both learned and experienced is encouraged (citing a paragraph of John of the Cross). For this reason each seminary is to have its own official spiritual director(s) besides the one(s) chosen personally by the seminarians.

Church buildings or chapels, prayer corners, monasteries, pilgrimages and shrines are all helpful in the life of prayer (2691), though the CCC notes that shrines are special places (2691). Prayer is the life of the heart renewed. It ought to animate us at every moment, lest we forget him who is our life and our all. But to do this, the CCC teaches us that we need to pray at particular moments with intensity and duration (2697). Hence the need will always exist in the seminary for fixed prayer periods. There are three major expressions of prayer: vocal, meditative and mental, but all have in common one characteristic: recollection of the heart or watchful attentiveness and dwelling in God's presence (2699).

By words, our prayer takes flesh (2700) and so vocal prayer is an essential element of the Christian life. Thus, Jesus taught a vocal prayer and raised his voice often in prayer (2701). It is readily accessible to all (2704). Even the body and senses and feelings need to get into prayer to give God the perfect homage which is his due (2702-03). Prayer is internalized to the extent that we become aware of him to whom we speak. Thus vocal prayer becomes an *initial form* of contemplative prayer (2704). This latter point is most important because the future priest will lead many vocal prayers and so must learn to contemplate in them simultaneously.

The Role of Meditation

Meditation is a quest using books or icons to help us understand the how and why of the Christian life (CCC 2705). To meditate on what we read helps us to make it our own by bringing it to bear on our own situation; here, we discover the movements that stir the heart and we must be able to discern them (2707). There are many methods of meditation, but method is only a guide (2707). Thought, imagination, emotion and desire to deepen our convictions of faith and conversion are engaged by meditating on the mysteries of Christ, using *lectio divina* or the Marian rosary (2708).

Mental prayer according to St. Teresa is a frequent solitary conversation with him who, as we know, loves us (2709). One must make time for the Lord with firm determination not to give up no matter what the trials or dryness one may encounter (2710). We may not always be able to meditate, but we can always drop our masks and turn our heart to him who loves us and hand ourselves over to him as an offering to be purified and transformed (2710-11).

Difficulties in Prayer and Contemplation According to the *Catechism*

Contemplation is a gaze, in faith, fixed on Jesus in his mysteries in order to love him more dearly and follow him more closely (CCC 2715). It listens to his word with attentiveness, in silent love since the Father speaks in silence (2717). It is a union with Christ's prayer, so that even the Eucharist and the meaning of Christ's life comes alive to us by active love from the Holy Spirit (2718) — but in the darkness of faith (2718-19). Likewise, prayer is both a gift of grace and a determined response on our part, that is, it requires effort (2725). We struggle against ourselves and the devil; we pray as we live and live as we pray, and so if we do not live according to Christ's spirit we can no longer pray habitually in his name (2725). The spiritual struggle of our new life of grace is inseparable from the struggle of prayer (Ibid.). All become discouraged because they think prayer comes only from themselves and not the Holy Spirit as well. They also sometimes think prayer is simply meant to reach mental emptiness or the enjoyment of ritual attitudes and words (2726). Hence it is clear why all need a leader in prayer and why the *Catechism* assigns that task especially to the hierarchical structure of the Church.

Prayer is valueless to a mentality of profit and production in that it appears to be a mere flight from the world. It is neither an escape from reality nor a divorce from life (2727). Prayer itself is a struggle to gain humility, confidence and perseverance. When our prayers leave us with dryness or sadness for not giving our all, disappointment about not being heard according to our will (2728), there is a temptation to abandon it whether in the seminary or later in the priesthood. Hence, the ongoing need for days of recollection, preached or silent before the Blessed Sacrament, if seminarians are to persevere for a lifetime of prayer.

The usual difficulties in prayer are distractions and the sometimes unsuccessful attempt to drive them away. They usually show us what we are attached to (legitimately or otherwise) and we should use them to awaken our preferential and predominant love for God (2729). From another point of view, prayer is a struggle against our possessive and dominating ego (2730). Another difficulty is dryness with no taste for spiritual thoughts (2731). The most common and hidden temptation to prayer is our lack of faith (2732). Another temptation is spiritual apathy or sloth, a kind of sadness due to lack of self-discipline, carelessness of heart leading to painful discouragement, most of which is due to presumption (2733), that is, thinking one can do everything in prayer (and ministry) on one's own. What we need is trust (2734). Perhaps we are simply using God as an instrument for the apostolate, or have failed to examine whether or not our prayer is acceptable to him (2735).

If faith rests on God's action in history, then prayer is cooperation with his providence, his plan of love for human beings (2738). It is a paradox, but we have ultimately to learn about the mysteries and secrets of prayer by persevering in prayer (2742)! We must remember that it is always possible to pray whether walking, buying or selling, and even cooking (2743), (and perhaps during boring lectures!). It is impossible to sin if we pray eagerly and invoke him often (2744 citing a thought of St. John Chrysostom). Therefore, it goes without saying: prayer and Christian life (here, particularly, seminary and priestly life) are inseparable for they concern the same love (2745).

Conclusion

In sum, St. Thomas Aquinas when speaking about friendship indirectly is helping all the Christian faithful to understand the depths of contemplation similar to spending time with one's friend. Likewise, he implicitly shows why we ministerial priests, members of the consecrated life, and laity, should all "waste" the time to pray, study and contemplate (these actions seen as an interpenetrating unity) the mysteries of God each day:

The beloved, as it were, remains continually in the one who loves him so that the lover uninterruptedly thinks of his friend, and inversely he who loves is by thought in his friend for he is not simply content to know superficially his friend, but applies himself to know him profoundly and in great detail. Thus, he penetrates as much as possible into his most intimate thoughts. For example, it is stated of the Holy Spirit — Who is the Love of God — that "He searches the profundity of God" (1 Cor 2:10). When it comes to the love of friendship, the lover makes his own the very joys and sufferings of his friend. It is as if he himself experienced these things in his friend. For this reason, it is proper for friends to want the same joys and sufferings. Likewise, he who loves, for the simple reason that he considers as his own that which has to do with this friend, seems to be in him and identifies himself with such a friend. Inversely, the friend is in him who loves him by the fact that he wills and acts in view of the friend whom he considers to be another self (ST I-II 28, 2).

Chapter Three

Study, A Quasi-Sacrament for the Priest

In the history of spirituality, there was a definite anti-intellectual trend found in the *Devotio Moderna* movement of the Netherlands in the fourteenth century.[1] As our new millennium continues, such a problem does not exist but rather the reverse: an over-reliance on the intellect's ability to fathom the contents of faith and morals which turns holy teaching into a mere academic exercise. What seems to be needed in this time of media and cyber explosion is a spirituality of study so that the intellectual can steer clear of the temptations that go with the desire to think about creation and the faith independently of God.

The spiritual life consists in cooperating with the Holy Spirit so that the graces and charisms offered by the Holy Spirit will pervade all of one's human acts. What this means is that virtues are established from within the situation one is in always from the motive of seeking the glory of God in one's particular vocation.[2] Yet another way of putting it conceptually is that spirituality means to seek and live by the grace of holiness offered to a person in any condition or state of life. As circumstances change, so one must adopt a stance looking to please or glorify God from the simplest to the most sublime responsibili-

---

[1] Jordan Aumann, O.P., *Christian Spirituality in the Catholic Tradition* (San Francisco: Ignatius Press, 1986), pp. 62-168.

[2] *Catechism of the Catholic Church*, 294; see also Antonio Royo, O.P., Jordan Aumann, O.P., *Theology of Christian Perfection* (Dubuque, Iowa: The Priory Press, 1962), pp. 23-26.

ties of one's state in life.[3] Moreover, what is absolutely essential for progress in the spiritual life is that one attempts to infuse into all intrinsically good and even indifferent acts (like barbecuing ribs) the spirit of charity in a more conscious way as well as doing what is possible to eliminate grave and even deliberate venial sins in every situation.

Faith Seeking Understanding Produces More Divine Love

When writing about the "missions" of the Son and the Holy Spirit to the baptized person, St. Thomas noted that any new knowledge that comes from faith is meant to "do" something to the human person:

> By grace the soul takes on a God-like form. That a divine person be sent to someone through grace, therefore, requires a likening to the person sent through some particular gift of grace. Since the Holy Spirit is Love, the likening of the soul occurs through the gift of charity and so the Holy Spirit's mission is accounted for by reason of charity. The Son in turn is the Word; not, however, just any word, but the **Word breathing love**.... Consequently not just any enhancing of the mind indicates being sent, but only that sort of enlightening that **bursts forth into love** (ST I 43, 5 ad 2).

What all this means is that the study or meditation or contemplation of sacred truth under the ordinary grace of the Holy Spirit should so enlighten one that any lights received stimulate acts of divine love for God and neighbor.

---

[3] Following the principles of St. Margaret Mary Alacoque, several saints go so far to say that they want to "console" the Sacred Heart by their lives. Ample evidence exists in the writings of St. Thérèse, St. John Vianney, and the Blesseds Jacinta and Francisco of Fatima fame.

Infused Charity: The Form or Inspirer of All the Virtues

It has been remarked that St. Thérèse of Lisieux said, "You can save a soul by picking up a needle." If this is true, what she meant was that in the spiritual life the infused divine love of God that one has in one's heart is more important than actual deeds done, because any ordinary act inspired by charity can merit graces for oneself and/or others.[4] Or better, someone washing a floor or a car may do so with greater charity/love than someone teaching a class in a university or writing a book.

If infused divine love is the mainstay of growing in a relationship with God, then it can inspire an ordinary act of study and/or the act of thinking since this activity is allied to the possession of natural and supernatural truth.[5] Truth is the goodness of the intellect and also a potential mover of the will depending upon its content. So then, on the natural level, if one's motives and circumstances are good, the act of study is morally good and virtuous. And, if one's principal motive is to please God and save souls and this is done in the state of sanctifying grace, then the simple act of studying can also be meritorious. However, if someone is studying for all the wrong motives such as love of self or self-glorification or even power over others and the like, then instead of being a virtue, it becomes a vice. St. Augustine said something similar when he wrote in his Rule: "For this is the peculiar feature of pride, that whereas every other kind of wick-

---

[4] CCC 2010. "Since the initiative belongs to God in the order of grace, *no one can merit the initial grace* of forgiveness and justification, at the beginning of conversion. Moved by the Holy Spirit and by charity, *we can then merit* for ourselves and for others the graces needed for our sanctification, for the increase of grace and charity, and for the attainment of eternal life. Even temporal goods like health and friendship can be merited in accordance with God's wisdom. These graces and goods are the object of Christian prayer. Prayer attends to the grace we need for meritorious actions."

[5] CCC 1827. "The practice of all the virtues is animated and inspired by charity, which "binds everything together in perfect harmony"; [105] it is the *form of the virtues*; it articulates and orders them among themselves; it is the source and the goal of their Christian practice. Charity upholds and purifies our human ability to love, and raises it to the supernatural perfection of divine love."

edness is exercised in the accomplishment of bad deeds, pride creeps stealthily in and destroys even good deeds."[6]

Study as a Vice

In his treatment of the vice of study, called by Aquinas *curiositas* (ST II-II 167, 1), he makes the point that discovering truth can be incidentally bad because of a bad consequence such as pride (*he could have also written here in the modern context about wasting time watching too much television or seeing too many films*) or when someone uses the truth in order to commit a sin. He also notes that certain inordinateness can occur in the desire for knowledge when someone studies "the less profitable" and this interferes with the studies "incumbent on their office." Second, some may even seek to gain knowledge from sinful sources like turning to the devil to foretell the future.[7] *Perhaps today, Thomas would have criticized scientists who seek knowledge by experimenting on human beings without their informed consent, and he probably would have been critical of people who waste time on the internet or use it for sinful purposes.* Third, a person may desire to know about nature without seeking to know about God. Finally, someone can seek to know things beyond his or her capacity and so easily fall into error.

In article two, the Angelic Doctor will add to the previous list that *curiositas* can lead one to seek knowledge which has no useful purpose and may serve to defeat it as, for example, using a contemporary illustration, the excessive watching of movies which distract from religious contemplation either because they are only interesting or entertaining and lack depth, or worse, lead one to commit acts of lechery or cruelty by watching certain

---

[6] *Rule of St. Augustine* as found in the *Book of Constitutions and Ordinations of the Order of Friars Preachers* (Rome: General Curia 1984), p. xxi.

[7] St. Thomas is also aware that one could seek knowledge from illicit sources such as fortune-tellers, tarot cards, and the like. See ST II-II 96, 6-8; 97, 1-4.

scenes (ad 2). He concludes that some types of knowledge can be evil due to "prying into the doings of others lead[ing] to detraction."

More examples come to mind after pondering Aquinas' teaching. For instance, if a priest so loves study that he ignores his other duties of hearing confessions and preparing his homilies, then such study in this case is not morally good. If a husband loves his scientific experiments or mathematical equations and rarely speaks with his children as a consequence, then such study is not morally good, even though good in itself as a fulfillment of the intellect of the scientist even if the results of his theories save lives.

It can also happen that someone obliged to study such as a Dominican student, or any student for the priesthood or a faculty member may not be virtuous in his study if he only reads theological books for their own sake, or memorizes certain reasoning processes simply to pass examinations, or worse, fails to contemplate lovingly over the truth discovered in them. For St. Thomas, theology especially is sacred or holy teaching which conclusions must be gazed upon, even relating the truth of other sciences to God's natural or supernatural revelation. The young theologian may unfortunately read books primarily for the pleasure of reading rather than for the work of memorizing and gleaning light about God and the things related to God for the salvation of others. This is why it is essential that the spirit of contemplative prayer also enter into the work of study of divine revelation, lest the theologian or the ordinary believer begin to think that his or her power of reasoning is greater than the faith they are trying to understand or fathom. Likewise, prayer must be at the heart of any religious contemplation so that doubts, confusions, and ignorance of faith do not overwhelm the person contemplating. In this way, the truth understood in mystery is seen as a gift of God rather than a creation of the theologian or any human mind flowing more from the spirit of presumption than from the spirit of prayer.

The Act of Study and "Studiositas"

Studying out of books or the book of nature or reflecting on experience has several parts: understanding the data of one's subject, judging its truthfulness, and contemplating its conclusions whether it be mathematics or political science, history or biology, philosophy or theology. Since study is a human act at least indifferent in itself caused by exercising the faculties of the intellect, memory and imagination, it can be part of a virtue or a vice, depending upon one's motives and circumstances.

So, it took St. Thomas Aquinas to discover a virtue surrounding the issue of study or the devotion to learning. He treats these matters under the over-arching virtue of temperance since spiritual pleasures are involved which must be "regulated" or directed by reason and faith. He calls the virtue of study *studiositas* which can be translated as "studiousness" which is also translated by the Blackfriars edition of the *Summa* as "devotion to learning" and its corresponding vice *curiositas* which is almost untranslatable since in the English-speaking world "curiosity" or "inquisitiveness" can also mean something good and even a synonym for "studiousness." In any case, every student whether of theology or chemistry who applies the mind rightly can sanctify the self and others by acting with *studiositas* linked to divine love insofar as he or she works at the desk trying to fathom a particular subject matter as part of his or her vocation. If the primary and immediate subject matter of study also happens to be God or the things of God, then the truth pondered over or contemplated will even more augment divine love, and quite often this divine love will usually augment a greater search for truth.

Contemplation of divine truth, then, is a special virtue related to the theological virtues and can also inspire the moral virtues. St. Thomas also teaches such when he says that when the moral virtues become more and more rooted in the human person, so the act of contemplation is facilitated (cf. ST II-II 182, 3). But to say that infused contemplation is the sole purpose of the spiritual life would be erroneous.

In his monumental work, *The Way of the Lord Jesus*,[8] Germain Grisez criticized the Augustinian over-emphasis with contemplation, as if it were the only virtue in the life of Christ. Rightly, Grisez speaks of Christian life as something wider. However, having made his point, he seemed to err too far saying that religious contemplation is a special form of religious life whereas St. Thomas' treatment in the *Summa* concerning the active and the contemplative life is about these subjects open to all Christians (cf. ST II-II 180-182). St. Thomas is again quite clear that moral virtues of lay, religious or clerics are at the root of contemplative virtue:

> Isidore says, *All vices must first be eradicated by the practice of good works in the active life, so that, the mind's eye being purified, one may advance to the contemplation of God in the contemplative life.* But all vices are uprooted only by the acts of the moral virtues. Consequently the acts of the moral virtues fit into the active life (ST II-II 182, 1 sed contra).

> Hence the practice of the active life (of virtue) is conducive to the contemplative life because it quells the internal passions from which arise the images that impede contemplation (ST II-II 182, 3).

In the Thomistic explanation, the reason why many do not live by the gifts of the Holy Spirit or possess infused contemplation (wisdom, understanding or knowledge) is not that they are only granted as favors for a few but that most are not yet advanced in virtue for God to act habitually this way in their souls. To live by the gifts of the Holy Spirit should be the normal and logical outcome of living the ordinary virtues in the first place. But unfortunately either by personal fault or psychological and in-

---

[8] Germain Grisez, *The Way of the Lord Jesus: Christian Moral Principles* (Chicago: Franciscan Herald Press, 1983), p. 772.

voluntary circumstances outside of their control, most Christians are not yet ready for such a habitual life of complete transformation by the Holy Spirit.

Prayer or Meditation?

Why is meditation as distinct from mental prayer so important for the person whose vocation is to study? St. Thomas has a great deal to say about this matter because it is so integral for the life of virtue. First it is important to look at meditation from the point of view of pleasure:

> …because every man finds delight when he has attained what he loves, it follows that the contemplative life terminates in delight, which is in the will, and this in its turn intensifies love (ST II-II 180, 1).

> We have seen that contemplation of truth is the greatest of all pleasures. We have seen too that every pleasure assuages pain. The contemplation of truth therefore assuages pain; and it does so the more, the more perfectly one loves wisdom. This is why men find joy in the midst of tribulation by contemplating the things of God and the happiness to come (ST I-II 38, 4).

Later in a similar article of II-II 180, Thomas makes the point that the will moves the intellect to seek the truth, sometimes out of love for things seen or investigated. For the celibate, this is important because giving up the pleasures of married and family life, he must still have some pleasures but of a higher kind to sublimate his life with.

More importantly, however, meditation/contemplation (for St. Thomas they seem to be like a movement toward and a restful delight which initiate or influence each other) stirs up that necessary virtue of religion called "devotion":

Clearly, however, the intrinsic or human cause of devotion is contemplation or meditation. Devotion is an act of the will by which a man promptly gives himself to the service of God. Every act of the will proceeds from some consideration of the intellect, since the object of the will is a known good; or as Augustine says, *willing proceeds from understanding*. Consequently, meditation is the cause of devotion since through meditation man conceives the idea of giving himself to the service of God (ST II-II 82, 3).

The Further Virtues in the Life of Study

St. Thomas recognizes that both meditation and contemplation can be initiated by the gifts of the Holy Spirit, something which cannot be legislated by either the Church or by any religious Rule of life. Yet in the *Code of Canon Law* 663 §1, we discover the following: "Contemplation of divine things and assiduous union with God in prayer is to be the first and foremost duty of all religious." How can this seeming contradiction be reconciled? Aquinas takes his teaching from Richard of St. Victor because it matches experience and common sense:

According to Richard of St. Victor, *cogitation* would seem to refer to the consideration of many things from which one intends to gather a simple truth. Consequently it can include sense perceptions for the knowledge of certain effects, also acts of the imagination, and the discursus of reasoning as well concerning the various signs of whatever will lead to a knowledge of certain effects, or whatever will lead to a knowledge of the truth which is sought. However, according to Augustine, any actual operation of the intellect can be called 'cogitation.'

Meditation would seem to refer to the process of reasoning from certain principles which arrive at the contemplation of some truth. According to Bernard, *consideration* means the same thing, although, according to Aristotle, every operation of the intellect is called *consideration.*

Contemplation, however, refers to a simple gaze upon a truth. Hence, Richard of St Victor states that *contemplation is the souls' penetrating and easy gaze on things perceived; meditation is the investigation of a mind occupied in the search of truth; cogitation is the concentration of a mind that is prone to wander* (ST II-II 180, 3 ad 1).

These various acts called cogitation, meditation and contemplation are within the power of the human person, though weakened somewhat by original sin. That is why in religious life, there is meant to be a spirit of silence and a daily routine to strengthen one's innate ability to think more deeply in the line of Richard of St. Victor's analysis. So then, whether one be in the library, one's room or the chapel or even the TV room, it is possible to be prayerfully contemplating some aspect of faith or in a state of meditative or even mental prayer.

In some traditions such as the Carmelite school, periods of mental prayer are called for, others such as the Jesuits or Sulpicians call these time periods, "meditation." In the Dominican tradition, study of sacred truth embraces both because sacred truth is meant to fire up charity, devotion to God and neighbor, as well as fostering prayer of different kinds, from petition to praise or to love.

What Does the *Catechism* Have to Say About Study?

The *Catechism of the Catholic Church* has the entire fourth pillar or section devoted to contemplative prayer based upon what reason and faith of the human person can do for itself in the spiritual life with the help of the grace of the Holy Spirit. From a certain point of view, the *Catechism* lacks a more complete treatment of contemplative study, though it hints at it in various numbers probably leaving that task up to theologians to articulate. Taking a look at the issue of study, the *Catechism* says:

> 2651. The tradition of Christian prayer is one of the ways in which the tradition of faith takes shape and grows, especially through **the contemplation and study of believers** who treasure in their hearts the events and words of the economy of salvation, and through their profound grasp of the spiritual realities they experience [DV 8].

Here, prayer is seen as the result of both contemplation and study but the *Catechism* also recognizes that one can also "experience" the spiritual realities as well. St. Thomas would say that these experiences would be due to the infused gifts of the Holy Spirit (not the charisms), especially wisdom, understanding or knowledge which are activated not by one's own personal efforts but by the will of the Holy Spirit alone and the human person consenting to his activations. Ordinary knowledge and understanding of the faith is a human mode of knowing but under the special instigation of the Holy Spirit, the human person is now under the divine mode of knowing.[9]

Another aspect of study in the *Catechism* is its synthesis of reading, meditation, mental prayer and infused contemplation from a quotation of Guigo the Carthusian:

---

[9] See Royo and Aumann, *Christian Perfection*, pp. 85-92.

2654. The spiritual writers, paraphrasing Matthew 7:7, summarize in this way the dispositions of the heart nourished by the word of God in prayer: "Seek in reading and you will find in meditating; knock in mental prayer and it will be opened to you by contemplation" [Guigo the Carthusian, *Scala Claustralium*: PL 184, 476C].

Again, one finds that the virtue of study is part of a much larger process in the spiritual life called meditation:

2705. Meditation is above all a quest. The mind seeks to understand the why and how of the Christian life, in order to adhere and respond to what the Lord is asking. The required attentiveness is difficult to sustain. We are usually helped by books, and Christians do not want for them: the Sacred Scriptures, particularly the Gospels, holy icons, liturgical texts of the day or season, writings of the spiritual fathers, works of spirituality, the great book of creation, and that of history — the page on which the "today" of God is written.

All of this effort made by the Christian to understand the many dimensions of the Christian life has to be a cluster of virtues both infused and natural. In the following number of the *Catechism*, we see that meditation makes what we study something of our own or something very personal:

2706. To meditate on what we read helps us to make it our own by confronting it with ourselves. Here, another book is opened: the book of life. We pass from thoughts to reality. To the extent that we are humble and faithful, we discover in meditation the movements that stir the heart and we are able to discern them. It is a question of acting truthfully in order to come into the light: "Lord, what do you want me to do?"

In addition, this "quest" leads the individual to understand the various movements that ordinarily go on in the depths of the soul. This process is traditionally called "discernment of the spirits" for which both St. John of the Cross and St. Ignatius of Loyola were famous for their abilities.

Finally, the *Catechism* attempts to show how the work of meditation is related to prayer and how prayer pours in its dynamism to meditation. It is clear for Thomists that the study of theology is meant to foster all that the *Catechism* says should be done in meditation:

> 2708. Meditation engages thought, imagination, emotion, and desire. This mobilization of faculties is necessary in order to deepen our convictions of faith, prompt the conversion of our heart, and strengthen our will to follow Christ. Christian prayer tries above all to meditate on the mysteries of Christ, as in lectio divina or the rosary. This form of prayerful reflection is of great value, but Christian prayer should go further: to the knowledge of the love of the Lord Jesus, to union with him.

Conclusion

For a priest or anyone wanting a deep spiritual life, to think of study as a mere game of the mind and having no bearing on the life of prayer is an illusion, sometimes propagated by false or incomplete spiritualities. It is as dangerous to study too much, as Thomas makes note, as it is to study not at all because of a certain contempt of this "little" virtue of *studiositas*. The key to opening up the treasure of divine truth is not exclusively to spend hours before the Blessed Sacrament and abandon study but to acquire this virtue of studiousness and integrate it with the theological virtues, and prayer before the Blessed Sacrament. When this happens, then a true spirituality of study is alive and active not only in an individual priest but also in religious communities and seminaries, dioceses, and even university faculties.

Chapter Four

The Hidden Troubles of the Priesthood: The Evil One

It is generally forgotten by Christians that one of the principal effects of our redemption by Christ's death and resurrection is the defeat of what St. John calls "the prince of this world" (Jn 14:30). What exactly does this mean? Does it mean that the devil is put out of existence so that he no longer functions? Or that he no longer tempts us? Many Christians think the answer is yes to these questions. Instead of seeing that human beings have to face a lifelong confrontation with the "deceiver," they think that the major problems of humankind are the evils of the body, the weakness of will, and ignorance of mind. Yet the Catholic faith is quite clear about it: "The reason the Son of God appeared was to destroy the works of the devil" (1 Jn 3:8). What does this mean?

The Liturgy and Spiritual Amnesia

On the first Sunday of Lent, the Church places before us the extraordinary battle of Jesus with the devil after he had spent forty days in the desert fasting. This is a timely reminder that the greatest temptation of the devil for the vast majority of believers is to lead the people of God either to conclude to his nonexistence or simply forget that he exists. Once the devil persuades anyone that he does not exist, it is very much easier for him to lead anyone astray, though slowly over a period of years.

It is much like having an "operative" or "mole" hidden in a government who is able to manipulate policy because his spying goes undetected. It is much easier to deny the existence of the devil than of God because there are so many more signs of God's existence than there are of the devil's. Only revelation teaches us that there is such a creature as Satan, the tempter.

How Does He Do It?

St. Thomas Aquinas teaches that the devil can neither take away free will, nor know what is going on in our minds, nor directly intervene in our spiritual life. But he can persuasively influence the imagination and emotions so as to lead the mind and heart astray. The devil tries by friendly persuasion to get us to believe that God is our real enemy in the sense that God gives us impossible laws and difficult vocations to fulfill. This is especially persuasive when the temptations to commit sexual sins seem overwhelming. It is easy to begin thinking that God has made too many impossible and arbitrary demands upon human nature.

Another temptation of the devil is to get us to believe as a result of sickness, tragedy and other setbacks, that God no longer loves or cares because he has forgotten us. This temptation is fueled by another illusion of the devil whereby we think that feeling the sweetness of God is equivalent to loving God or a sure sign that he loves us. Further, everything going our way in terms of riches, fame, power over others and the like, is a sure sign to the deluded of the love of God. So when reverses come our way, it is easy to believe that God has abandoned us, and nourishing those thoughts (false meditations and contemplations really) leads to abandoning God. As a result, some no longer go to Mass or confession or spend time in authentic prayer, meditation and contemplation.

Yet another temptation of the devil consists in persuading people to form their consciences by inventing their own principles of morality instead of depending upon God's revelation. As the *Catechism* explains concerning the temptation of Adam and Eve:

> 398. In that sin man preferred himself to God and by that very act scorned him. He chose himself over and against God, against the requirements of his creaturely status and therefore against his own good. Created in a state of holiness, man was destined to be fully "divinized" by God in glory. Seduced by the devil, he wanted to "be like God," but "without God, before God, and not in accordance with God."

The way of morality presupposes the desire for happiness, or fulfillment by self-transcendence. But self-transcendence is only achieved by following a way of life based upon the natural and revealed norms of human action; these when followed lead to authentic fulfillment through virtues both moral and theological. To become fair-minded, self-possessed, tough-hearted in the face of obstacles, and wise in practical life as well as faith-filled, hopeful and charitable, one must depend upon God's grace and follow his wise and loving will as it is revealed by sacred scripture, and sacred tradition as taught by the sacred magisterium. The devil therefore attempts to convince people that they can eliminate certain norms and invent others which they erroneously think can lead them to happiness in this life even to a heaven of their own making in the next.

An Odd Aftermath of Vatican II

The denial of the existence of the devil among theologians during the late 1960's and 1970's prompted a magisterial document entitled *Christian Faith and Demonology* which was published on July 10, 1975 by the ordinary authority of the Sacred Congregation for the Doctrine of the Faith (without however

the signature of the prefect of the Congregation or the appro-
bation of the Pope, Paul VI). Rich in historical and scriptural
references, this document shows beyond question of a doubt that
the Church has always believed in the existence of the devil as a
force which must be reckoned with in the daily life of the Christian. *Christian Faith and Demonology* begins with some interesting cautions:

> The many forms of superstition, obsessional preoccu-
> pation with Satan and the demons, and the different
> kinds of worship of them or attachment to them have
> always been condemned by the Church.[1] It would
> therefore be incorrect to hold that Christianity, for-
> getful of the universal Lordship of Christ, had at any
> time made Satan the privileged subject of its preach-
> ing, transforming the Good News of the risen Lord
> into a message of terror. Speaking to the Christians
> of Antioch, St. John Chrysostom declared: "It cer-
> tainly gives us no pleasure to speak to you of the devil,
> but the teaching which this subject gives me the op-

---

[1] The Church's firmness with regard to superstition finds an early explanation in
the severity of the Mosaic Law, even though the latter was not formally motivated
by the connection of superstition with demons. Thus Exodus 22:18 condemned
the sorceress to death without explanation. Leviticus 19:26 and 31 prohibited
magic, astrology, necromancy and divination; Leviticus 20:27 added the calling
up of spirits. Deuteronomy 18:10-11 summed this up by proscribing soothsayers,
astrologers, magicians, sorcerers, charmers, those who summoned up ghosts or spirits and those who consulted the dead. In the Europe of the early Middle Ages, a
large number of pagan superstitions still flourished, as is testified by the sermons
of St. Caesareus of Arles and of St. Eligius, the *De Correctione Rusticorum* of Martin of Braga, the contemporary lists of superstitions (cf. PL 89, 810-818) and the
penitential books. The First Council of Toledo (DS 205) and the Council of Braga
(DS 459) both condemned astrology. Similarly the letter of Pope St. Leo the Great
to Turibius of Astorga (DS 283). Rule IX of the Council of Trent forbade works
of chiromancy, necromancy, etc. (DS 1859). Magic and sorcery alone evoked a
large number of papal Bulls (Innocent VIII, Leo X, Adrian VI, Gregory XV and
Urban VIII), and many decisions of regional synods. For hypnotism and spiritual-
ism see in particular the letter of the Holy Office of August 4, 1856 (DS 2823-
2825).

portunity to expound is of the greatest use to you."[2] In fact it would be an unfortunate error to act as if history had already been accomplished and the Redemption had obtained all its effects, without there being any further need to conduct the combat spoken of by the New Testament and the masters of the spiritual life.

This study then proceeds to show that there is massive evidence from the New Testament (especially the contradictory teachings on this question by the Pharisees and Sadducees, the two major religious groups at the time of Christ), to the Fathers of the Church and Popes all leading up to the Fourth Lateran Council of the thirteenth century, which demonstrate a fundamental teaching on the existence of the devil. This Council merely sums up this teaching when it proclaims in a Creed:

> We firmly believe and simply confess... one principle of the universe: the Creator of all things visible and invisible, spiritual and corporeal, who by His omnipotence from the beginning of time created all things from nothing, both spiritual and corporeal, namely, the angels and the world, then the human creature, which belongs in a certain way to both, for it is composed of spirit and of body. **For the devil and the other demons were created naturally good by God, but it is they who by their own action made themselves evil.** As for man, he sinned at the instigation of the devil.[3]

It seems rather strange that theologians shortly after Vatican II would dispute the doctrine of the devil when it was again reaffirmed at this Council. Hence *Christian Faith and Demonology* continues:

---

[2]   *De Diabolo Tentatore*, Homil. II, 1, PG 49, 257-258.
[3]   *Conciliorum Oecumenicorum Decreta*, ed. I.S.R., Bologna 1973, p. 230; DS 800.

It is for this reason that the Second Vatican Council, which concerned itself more often with the present condition of the Church than with creation, did not fail to warn against the activity of Satan and the demons. Once more, as at Florence and Trent, it recalled, with the Apostle, that Christ "takes us out of the power of darkness."(104) Summarizing Scripture in the manner of St. Paul and the book of Revelation, the Constitution *Gaudium et Spes* stated that our history, universal history, "is a hard struggle against the powers of darkness, a struggle begun with the beginning of the world and one which will continue, as the Lord says, until the last day." Elsewhere, Vatican II repeated the admonitions of the letter to the Ephesians to "put on the armor of God so as to resist the wiles of the devil." For, as the same Constitution reminds the laity, "we have to fight against the rulers of this dark world, against the spirits of evil." It is not surprising finally to note that the same Council, wishing to emphasize that the Church is truly the Kingdom of God already begun, appeals to the miracles of Jesus and for this purpose makes explicit reference to His exorcisms. It was on this occasion, in fact, that Jesus made the celebrated statement, "then the Kingdom of God has come upon you."

In conclusion, the same document sums up the reason why the existence of the devil was never solemnly defined by the Magisterium:

Briefly then, the Church's position in regard to demonology is clear and firm. It is true that in the course of the centuries the existence of Satan and of the devils has never in fact been the object of an explicit declaration of her magisterium. The reason for this is that the question was never posed in these terms. Both heretics and the faithful, basing their respective positions on Sacred Scripture, were in agreement in recognizing the existence of Satan and the devils and their main misdeeds. This is why, when the reality of the devil is called into question today, it is to the constant and universal belief of the Church and to its main source, the teaching of Christ, that one must appeal, as has been stated. It is in fact in the teaching of the Gospel and as something at the heart of the faith that the existence of the demonic world is shown to be a dogmatic datum. The present-day unease which we described at the beginning does not therefore call into question a secondary element of Christian thinking; it is a question, rather, of the constant belief of the Church, of her manner of conceiving redemption and, at the root source, it goes against the very consciousness of Jesus. This is why, when his Holiness Pope Paul VI spoke recently of this "terrible, mysterious and frightening reality" of evil, he could assert with authority: "he who refuses to recognize its existence, or whoever makes of it a principle in itself which does not have, like every creature, its origin in God, or who explains it as a pseudo-reality, a conceptual and imaginary personification of the unknown causes of our ills, departs from the integrity of biblical and ecclesiastical teaching." Neither exegetes nor theologians can neglect this caution.

The Devil and Human Freedom

Even though the Church believes that the devil exists, this does not mean that falling into sin can be said to be primarily caused by the devil, so as to rule out our own personal responsibility:

Let us therefore repeat that by underlining today the existence of demonic reality the Church intends neither to take us back to the dualistic and Manichaean speculations of former times, nor to propose some rationally acceptable substitute for them. She wishes only to remain faithful to the Gospel and its demands. It is clear that she has never allowed man to rid himself of his responsibility by attributing his faults to the devil. The Church did not hesitate to oppose such escapism when the latter manifested itself, saying with St. John Chrysostom: "It is not the devil but men's own carelessness which causes all their falls and all the ills of which they complain."

In other words, temptation does not mean that people lack freedom in the face of the evil counselor's attempts to persuade them to do wrong. As the document of the Sacred Congregation makes clear even further:

It is to faith in fact that the apostle St. Peter leads us back when he exhorts us to resist the devil, "strong in faith." Faith teaches us that the reality of evil "is a living, spiritual being, perverted and corrupting" (124). Faith can also give us confidence, by assuring us that the power of Satan cannot go beyond the limits set by God. Faith likewise assures us that even though the devil is able to tempt us, he cannot force our consent. Above all, faith opens the heart to prayer, in which it finds its victory and its crown. It thus enables us to triumph over evil through the power of God.

Finally the document teaches us that our understanding of why God permits the devil to do what he does remains somewhat of a mystery (later on the *Catechism of the Catholic Church* will give us more light on the matter):

It certainly remains true that the demonic reality, attested to in the concrete by what we call the mystery of evil, remains an enigma surrounding the Christian life. We scarcely know any better than the apostles knew why the Lord permits it, nor how He makes it serve His designs. It could be, however, that, in our civilization obsessed with secularism that excludes the transcendent, the unexpected outbreaks of this mystery offer a meaning less alien to our understanding. They force man to look further and higher, beyond the immediate evidence. Through their menace, which stops us short, they enable us to grasp that there exists a beyond which has to be deciphered, and then to turn to Christ in order to hear from Him the Good News of salvation graciously offered to us.

The Catechism's Doctrine

The *Catechism* (391-395; 2850-2858) has much more to say about this question of the "evil one" which in many ways goes beyond the teaching of the Congregation's document of 1975 because the latter was the theological labor of one or several theologians. The *Catechism* asserts that the devil's power is not infinite and even though he can cause injury "he cannot stop God's reign" (CCC 395). God permits him to instigate many kinds of evil which are somehow part of God's loving plan (395), even though such providence does not always appear, to those weak in faith, to be loving or even wise. But then neither does a piece of unleavened bread appear even remotely to be the body of Christ once it is validly consecrated by a priest.

What Does the Devil Normally Do to Lead People Astray?

Since the devil is called the "seducer," we need to pose the question: how does he lead the human person astray? St. Thomas Aquinas masterfully tells us that the devil tries to persuade us to consent to sin through the power of rationalization or blandishments (cf. ST I 111, 2 ad 2; 114, 1-5; *De Malo* 3, 3-5) that is, the devil tries to get us to deceive ourselves in the act of choosing an apparent good (and, I would add, by avoiding the pursuit of a real good because it seems to us to be an evil). In gently inciting people to turn their attention to a particularly attractive sin, Satan tries to catch everyone in the false belief that the sin in question is at least not all that bad; and, that seeming good which is manifested by an appearance of a delightful outcome (which one should be rejecting or foregoing in order to obey God), is still very needful for personal fulfillment. In any case, the evil one is the expert at getting us to evade reality.

Therefore, the need to develop a prayer life so that each and all can face reality as it is and not as anyone desires it to be. It is not by accident that the greatest prayer given by the Lord Jesus is the Our Father, which ends "Lead us not into temptation but deliver us from evil." Of course, the Father does not "lead" anybody into sin but if someone chooses a sinful action, he lets that person have the freedom and the consequences of that choice. Hence, the *Catechism* tells us, the believer can fathom a purpose behind the difficulty of temptation:

> 409. This dramatic situation of "the whole world [which] is in the power of the evil one" makes man's life a battle:
>
> The whole of man's history has been the story of dour combat with the powers of evil, stretching, so our Lord tells us, from the very dawn of history until the last day. Finding himself in the midst of the battlefield man has to struggle to do what is right, and it is at

great cost to himself, and aided by God's grace, that he succeeds in achieving his own inner integrity.

The Witness of the Lord's Prayer

In the section of the *Catechism* that comments on the Our Father (2850-56), there is a wealth of material to ponder upon in relation to the devil. We are reminded that Satan is the evil one who "throws himself across God's plan" for us; that he is a liar, a murderer from the beginning. But as 1 John 5:18-19 teaches, the evil one does not touch someone born of God. But this baptismal gift of lived filiation is not something automatic. The victory of Jesus over the evil one presumes our cooperation. The *Catechism* (2852) gives us a beautiful quotation from St. Ambrose to help us focus on the meaning of this particular aspect of our faith:

> The Lord who has taken away your sin and pardoned your faults also protects you and keeps you from the wiles of your adversary the devil, so that the enemy who is accustomed to leading into sin, may not surprise you. One who entrusts himself to God does not dread the devil. "If God is for us, who is against us."

The victory of Jesus is ours when we pray, trust in God, and use the faith of the Catholic Church to guide us in our way of life which is not a mere matter of a chosen lifestyle, for morality is not a "style" like a set of clothes. Of course, once we abandon prayer and entertain doubts about the deposit of faith and moral teaching (which is really faith in action), then we permit the devil to gently persuade us to fall into the sins that are closest to our weak points. Worse, of course, we let him deceive us into thinking that our sins are no longer sins, and this leads to the hardening of one's heart (CCC 1859, 1864).

The victory of Christ is such that he does not allow the devil to test us beyond our capacity (CCC 2848; 1 Cor 10:13). The Lord Jesus entirely defeated the devil for us but he wants us to share his triumph by enduring temptation and choosing him through acts of faith, hope and love. As the *Catechism* wisely teaches:

> 2847. The Holy Spirit makes us discern between trials, which are necessary for the growth of the inner man, and temptation, which leads to sin and death. We must also discern between being tempted and consenting to temptation. Finally, discernment unmasks the lie of temptation, whose object appears to be good, a "delight to the eyes" and desirable, when in reality its fruit is death.

> God does not want to impose the good, but wants free beings.... There is a certain usefulness to temptation. No one but God knows what our soul has received from him, not even we ourselves. But temptation reveals it in order to teach us to know ourselves, and in this way we discover our evil inclinations and are obliged to give thanks for the goods that temptation has revealed to us.

The temptations caused by the devil then become instruments or occasions of God's intervention on behalf of those that seek him from their hearts.

Finally, we discover from the *Catechism* that the last petition of the Our Father, "Deliver us from all evil," is ultimately related to the devil himself, the evil one:

> 2851. In this petition, evil is not an abstraction, but refers to a person, Satan, the Evil One, the angel who opposes God. The devil (dia-bolos) is the one who

"throws himself across" God's plan and his work of salvation accomplished in Christ.

2852. "A murderer from the beginning... a liar and the father of lies," Satan is "the deceiver of the whole world (Jn 8:44; Rev 12:9)." Through him sin and death entered the world and by his definitive defeat all creation will be "freed from the corruption of sin and death." Now "we know that anyone born of God does not sin, but He who was born of God keeps him, and the evil one does not touch him (1 Jn 5:18-19)."

With the two documents treated above, the Catholic community (and priests in particular) has sufficient data to keep itself aware of this secondary faith fact and reality of the devil, notwithstanding the apparent silence of the clergy on this ordinary content of faith. Still, average Catholics (and even priests) may become the objects of ridicule and be accused of "fundamentalism" by dissenters within particular churches, elements which seem to influence the clergy so much in our times. The devil uses these elements to persuade the people of God to veer away from the truth of revelation and accept error as normative. This permission of God likewise is part of a loving plan that will only reveal itself in the beatific vision. For now, one needs vigilance and trust or as it has been said by Peter, "Resist him, solid in your faith" (1 P 5:9a).

Chapter Five

Pride: The Enemy Within

In the English language, there are two senses denoted by the word "pride." A positive sense is seen in the statement such as, "I take pride in my family, my diocese, country, school, team, and work." What this means is that I recognize and pay or feel honor, or recognize with affection the goodness or qualities which I find in these realities. A darker and more traditional meaning of the word "pride" is used to refer to a great enemy of the life of the spirit. Combating its influence is essential in one's personal life in order not to end up with Satan's "I will not serve" complex.

In the Rule of St. Augustine, readers are warned that pride can enter even good works and so one must be on the lookout for it in one's soul:

> For this is the peculiar feature of pride, that whereas every other kind of wickedness is exercised in the accomplishment of bad deeds, pride creeps stealthily in and destroys even good deeds.[1]

Moral theologians at one time were more careful to warn their students that for an action to be morally upright and good, the three fonts of morality had to coalesce together: the moral object of an act, (that is, its scope or whatness), the due circumstances, and the intention (cf. CCC 1755-56). Spiritual theology is very concerned with the third of these fonts, the ultimate

---

[1] *Rule of St. Augustine* as found in the *Constitutions and Ordinations of the Order of Friars Preachers.*

intention of seeking the glory of God and his kingdom in living one's life when aiming at accomplishing virtuous deeds.[2] The moralist for his part is concerned primarily with expounding the object of a moral action, and also, waking up a person's prudence to see that the circumstances are properly ordered so that a particular deed is done with reason and proportion under faith. Wearing a bathing suit, for example, while not intrinsically wrong, does not find its proper due circumstance at Mass in a Cathedral, and so, being an imprudent act, would not be morally upright. We turn now to St. Thomas Aquinas to give us a few tips on the question of how pride enters the spiritual life.

For St. Thomas it is clear that the human person has a keen desire for excellence, which can come under the virtue of magnanimity. "Magnanimity implies a certain aspiration of spirit to great things" (ST II-II 129, 1). There is nothing wrong in the desire to be like God in that respect ("Be perfect as your heavenly Father is perfect," Mt 5:48). The problem is not so much in the desire as such; rather it is in the obtaining of a particular excellence, be it moral virtue, honors from winning a chess tournament, a doctorate in Urdu or holiness itself. The Second Vatican Council openly called the laity to holiness, so much so that it is almost trite these days to state, "Everyone has a vocation to holiness" (cf. CCC 2013). But that achievement requires great and small efforts. Any minor responsibility can bring about holiness, from playing Beethoven well to mowing a lawn correctly to picking up a needle (as St. Thérèse might say) or even moderately sipping a glass of bourbon so long as done with great love for God. The same would be true of more difficult actions such as saving a life, ministering to the sick, or spending hours daily in contemplation of God or the Eucharist. Good and indifferent acts, simple or difficult, done with and under the theological virtue of charity and prudence, can glorify God and merit

---

[2] Jordan Aumann, O.P., *Spiritual Theology* (Huntington, IN: Our Sunday Visitor and Sheed and Ward, 1980), 36-49.

grace for self and others. Sometimes, we do not achieve excellence in a particular endeavor because we do not want to suffer the pain or do the work due to our laziness or satisfaction with mediocrity. Prayer, meditation, and contemplation especially require effort, which must accompany the achievement of any kind of excellence in virtue, as an essential condition. Even though we are promised a great deal of help from God, we must pray for this help as a sign that we really do choose to depend or rely upon God. Aquinas reminds us:

> To strive after ambitious objects is contrary to humility when it issues from confidence in your own abilities, not from confidence in divine help, especially since the more one humbles oneself before God, the more one is lifted up before him (ST II-II 161, 3 ad 2).

Additionally, many may strive for a particular virtue such as patience or chastity as if it were the ultimate end of their lives rather than as a subordinate end toward seeking the glory and love of God. When this happens, quite often the inspiration and the thrust is not from divine love but a very familiar kind of self-love wanting to appropriate a virtue for its own sake in order to feel good, and perhaps to gloat over one's neighbor's lack thereof. When that takes place, pride dethrones the true reasons for achieving virtue in the first place, and may give rise to one of its lieutenants, such as the seven capital vices. For Thomas, pride is an overarching capital vice penetrating the other seven. For other authors, pride is conflated with vain-glory.

When analyzing pride as a sin, St. Thomas gives a superb objection defending pride even to the point of calling it a virtue:

> Further, to desire to be like God is no sin, for every creature is charged with this appetite for the realization of its optimum. Especially is it becoming to a

rational creature made to God's image and likeness. Now it is said in Prosper's *Sentences* that pride is love of one's own excellence, which reflects God who is supremely excellent. And so Augustine says, "Pride imitates exaltedness, though you, God are alone exalted above all" (ST II-II 162, 1 obj 2).

In answering this brilliant objection, Thomas describes the sin of pride as that whereby "a man's will aims above what he really is; hence Isidore notes that 'a man is said to be proud because he wills to appear higher than he is,' and he who wills to overstep his bounds is proud. Right reason (however) requires that a man should reach out to what is proportionate to him...." Thomas will note that quite often people "pride themselves" in possessing a plethora of material things (ad 1) which in contemporary language could mean that some persons think that the more they possess, the better they are. Here it becomes clear why true self-knowledge is the condition for humility, the antidotal virtue which fights against the sin of pride.

Pride then is a craving for excellence out of sync with what is reasonable, and so is a bad imitation of God because the proud person "hates being equal with [his] fellows... but wills to dominate them as taking his [God's] place" (ad 2). What this means is that arrogance leads people steadily to desire to achieve control over others or unreasonably to desire to be in charge of human or ecclesiastical affairs for all the wrong reasons. Pride can even look like the virtue of magnanimity because it "reaches out for greatness but not in conformity to reason's judgment of one's abilities" (ad 3), and, I would add, God's particular will for this or that particular person. Perhaps some priests fall into this trap by wanting to do better works without the requisite talents or because the superiors who appointed them merely project their own talents or lack thereof onto them because of human friendship.

In II-II 162, 2, Thomas shows that pride can also be looked at conceptually as a vice with its own special interest, namely an "inordinate appetite for one's own superiority." Any sin can be prompted by such a spirit and quite often be repulsed by "the divine law which keeps a man from sinning" because some proud persons want no limits to their behavior (freedom of choice without boundaries). Harkening back to the seventies, how often it was said by some that the Church could not tell people what to do in their bedrooms. However, Aquinas will go on and say that not all sins are caused by pride, because some come from ignorance or weakness and not from malice.

In II-II 162, 3 ad 1, Thomas gives a brilliant psychological insight into pride in terms of the student who struggles for truth:

> A truth may be known in two ways, as merely thought about and as really experienced. Pride hinders purely theoretical knowledge by removing its cause, that is, the proud submit their minds to learn from no one, neither God nor man, in order to come to the truth.

This helps explain why there can be such resistance in the human spirit to faith-knowledge, as well as a refusal of students to listen to ordinary instructors, theologians, the sacred Magisterium, or even the failure of children to take in the wisdom of their parents. Pride can infect anyone's attitude such that a man or a woman refuses to ask others for advice in the practical order of things, or insight in the speculative order of reality. Further, to learn the truth about reality takes humble listening to others which is a kind of prudence called docility. In his treatment of prudence, Thomas explains how pride can interfere with good decision making:

> Nature makes us apt to be taught, as it makes us apt for the other qualities of prudence, yet to be generously docile calls for much effort, that a person who carefully, frequently, and respectfully attends to the teachings of men of weight, and neither neglects them

out of laziness nor *despises them out of pride* (emphasis mine) (ST II-II 49, 4 ad 2).

Aquinas is careful to observe that "even people in authority ought themselves to be tractable sometimes, for... in matters of prudence no one is wholly self-sufficient." This is the real reason why canon law requires bishops and priests to seek counsel before making certain decisions affecting a diocese or parish. However, Thomas pushes even further:

> But knowledge of the truth as really experienced through love with it is directly blocked by pride, for by hugging their own excellence, the proud grow bored with the excellence of truth itself (II-II 162, 3 ad 1).

He quotes Gregory the Great who asserts that proud people are not able to experience the sweetness of knowing and the relishing that accompanies seeing the truth of reality. This may also explain why many refuse to spend time contemplating divine truth either through study or in prayer such as the rosary. Also, teachers of all grades know that quite often it can be the case that students who do very well in school work and know the "answers" fail to savor truth, while others who may receive lower grades rejoice in their new penetration into their particular field of endeavor.

Thomas again articulates his thought when he states that a desire for one's own superiority pushes one to contribute to an "exaggerated self-esteem" with the deleterious consequence of "dwelling on other people's failings" (II-II 162, 3 ad 2). Again following Gregory, Thomas will say, based upon observation of people (perhaps his own Dominican community!), that pride leads to boasting about "qualities one does not possess" or imagining one has a gift from oneself, or if thinking profoundly about some aspect of reality is a gift from God, "believing one deserves it." These can all cause the bad habit of "looking down on others and wishing to appear singularly good." How often have priests wanted to become bishops and superiors for all these wrong reasons!

From another perspective, *Summa* II-II 162, 5 also suggests that the "root of pride" is "somehow not being subject to God and his rule." This is another way of saying that one person exceeds unreasonably his desire for excellence even though he does not have the requisite talents for a particular goal or aim for the work in question. In its deeper stages, pride ultimately becomes a kind of "contempt of God" either by not relying on his help or eventually hating God in some way.

Now, applying all these insights to the sin of Adam, Aquinas explains that the first sin was the unreasonable coveting of a likeness of God:

> Proto-man sinned principally in wanting to be like God in knowing good and evil as the serpent insinuated, so that he might determine for himself by his own natural powers what was right or wrong for him to do, or even that he might foresee for himself his future destiny for weal or woe. He sinned secondarily in desiring God's likeness in his own powers of action, so that of his own capabilities he might achieve happiness.... Indeed both devil and man wanted to be equal with God in some respect; each scorned the order of divine government by choosing to rely on himself instead (ST II-II 163, 2).

Here we find several examples that are very contemporary. The first one is the false view that anyone can determine for himself what is right and wrong by his free choice. The second is that conscience has no relationship to the objective truth and has no teacher who can correct it. The third is that a Catholic can trump the Magisterium's teaching if feelings and intuitions indicate that the Church's official teaching is wrong.

All of these possibilities reject the way the divine/human

government of the Church works because the vice of pride skews the judgment of the mind. This problem also raises other problems in the spiritual life that requires a special effort to combat "rash" judgments and decisions not only about one's capabilities, but equally important, about the virtues of others with whom we live. In Thomas' treatment on "passing judgment" he says the following:

> Our Lord's words forbid rash judgment, which, according to Augustine, is about secret motions of the heart and other uncertain things. Or according to Hilary, they forbid us judging divine things which, since they are above us, we ought to believe, not adjudicate. Or according to Chrysostom, they forbid criticism from bitterness of spirit, not benevolence (ST II-II 60, 2 ad 1).

Perhaps more difficult than fasting, discovering these negative tendencies (which ordinarily flow from pride) requires an interior fight against assenting to and acting upon the quick flashes of false intuition, which are frequently projections of oneself according to Aquinas. This fight will have certain implications for charity:

> According to Cicero a suspicion is an ill opinion founded on slight indications. It comes about from three causes. First, from a man being bad himself; conscious of his own wickedness, he is prone to think evil of others.... Second, from being ill-disposed towards another; when a man hates or despises another, or is angry with him or envious of him, he is swayed by slight signs to think evil of him, for everyone readily believes what he wants to believe. Third, by long experience; Aristotle remarks how *old people are very suspicious, for they have often experienced the faults of others* (II-II 60, 3).

Perhaps these comments of Aquinas help explain why vocation directors and some spiritual directors in seminaries may have rejected some students for the priesthood. Holding traditional views was seen by some to be a sign that a candidate was not fit to be flexible in the modern priestly ministry; this is a rash judgment based upon prejudice.

Thomas then asks: *should a person be given the benefit of the doubt?* In his replies to two objections, he will give some answers that are profound and again related to the issue of pride indirectly:

> He who interprets doubts in the more favorable sense may happen to be mistaken more often than not. All the same, to err frequently through thinking well of an unworthy man is better than to err less frequently through thinking ill of a worthy man, for in the second case an injustice is inflicted, but not in the first (II-II 60, 4 ad 1).

In judging about men, however, it is their good or evil which is the main point, inasmuch as they are held in honor or reproach in consequence, unless there be manifest evidence to the contrary. We may be mistaken, but that spells no evil to our intellect, for it is no part of its perfection at present to know the truth of individual and contingent things; but rather it shows kindly feeling.

Now the problem with the proud person who thinks too highly of himself and less highly of others in proximity is that he is almost forced into making many rash judgments about other people in order to raise himself above others. This, in turn, whittles away at charity, which should cause one to see Christ in others. Instead, these harsh judgments dispose one toward hatred, envy, lack of mercy, or simple neglect of friendliness.

On the other hand, common sense indicates that life requires many judgment calls based upon the observation of other people's external behavior, while not necessarily their human intentions. We can ultimately judge at most that certain actions are *apparent* mortal sins since we cannot know a person's soul, although we can determine objectively that some actions are gravely unjust.[3] It is important to note that there is no sin called "judgmental"; this is a modern notion that negative judgments of others is somehow condemned by Christ. On the contrary, it would not be sinful to judge that I have gravely harmed someone's well-being by deliberately burning his house down. He would not sin against charity if he called the police and had me arrested and arraigned for doing such a vicious act, especially if he can prove it.

St. Thomas has more to say about how pride can affect the judgment of others when he speaks about the sin of ambition:

> The desire for recognition therefore can be unbalanced in three ways. First a man can seek recognition of an excellence which he does not possess; which means seeking more than one's true share of recognition. Secondly, he can desire honor for himself without acknowledgment to God. Thirdly, his desire can rest content with recognition itself, without applying it to the service of others. But ambition denotes an unbalanced desire for recognition, and so clearly it is always a sin (ST II-II 131, 2).

Or, in other words, the unreasonable desire for recognition is the child of an unreasonable desire for excellence.

In discussing ambition and humility, Thomas asserts:

> To strive after ambitious objects is contrary to humility when it issues from confidence in your own abilities, not from confidence in divine help, especially since the more one humbles oneself before God the

---

[3]   Germain Grisez, *The Way of the Lord Jesus: Living A Christian Life*, Vol. 2 (Quincy, IL: Franciscan Press, 1993), 227-232.

more one is lifted up before him (ST II-II 161, 3 ad 1).

So, when pride rules, prayer becomes less and less operative in one's life since self-reliance becomes more dynamic than striving for the grace to do God's will.

Another sin deeply related to pride is the sin of presumption. Thomas gives the basis for this sin in persons who actively lobby for positions of higher authority falsely thinking they are capable of heroic deeds:

> Presumption does seem to imply a certain excessiveness of life, the object of which is some good, difficult but possible to attain. The element of possibility, where men are concerned, may be either in terms of a person's own capacities or of the divine power alone. Presumption can arise because of a lack of balance in regard to either grounds for hope (ST II-II 21, 1).

Again, after these general considerations, the Angelic Doctor considers the problem of desiring any office in order to be above others:

> Because of the eminence of their position recognition is due to men who are established in high office. In this sphere an unbalanced desire for high office is a characteristic of ambition. For if a person sought such office unreasonably, not for the purpose of recognition but because he aspired to a right use of it beyond his powers, he would be presumptuous rather than ambitious (II-II 36, 2 ad 2).

We shall see in chapter eight that growing in charity is more important than seeking higher offices in the Church or even "better" apostolic activities associated with more difficult works or responsibilities. What ultimately counts in the spiritual life is not the amount or difficulties of the toil to be expended but the depth of one's divine love manifested in whatever ministry flows from the priestly office. Quite often, hidden behind a desire for more authority and power over others, is an escape from the true challenge of the spiritual life which is usually, but not exclusively, to expand not outwardly in a greater diversity of works, but first, and more profoundly, in deeper desires for the purity of divine love lived more under the gifts of the Holy Spirit than in works accomplished predominantly by reason and faith. As Thomistic theologians of the spiritual life have articulated, living in the divine mode rather than the human mode of virtue, or better still, living the mystical way rather than the ascetical way, is the summit of the journey of the spiritual life on earth to which all should strive. St. John of the Cross puts it differently when he says that pure love of God is worth more than an abundance of works with imperfect love.[4] Yet in fact, the heroic virtues and their corresponding deeds, including great works, emerge not by sheer force of will power but primarily from the gifts of the Holy Spirit who energizes the soul for great works such as hours in the confessional, or at the desk writing books, or in governing a religious institute or diocese in some capacity.

Conclusion

In this short treatment of the sin of pride through the eyes of St. Thomas, spiritual directors can see the damage pride does to the individual, and historians know the damage it has done to the Church. Professors turning away from the Magisterium, superiors thinking they know better than the Church, pastors becoming laws unto themselves, priests and religious abandon-

---

[4] John of the Cross, *Living Flame*, from *The Collected Works of John of the Cross*, Kieran Kavanaugh, O.C.D. and Ottilio Rodriquez, O.C.D., eds. (Washington, DC: ICS Publications, 1991), p. 642.

ing the life of prayer for the ego thrills of personal praise, honor and glory from the media, or their adoring flocks or confreres lead to one certain conclusion: pride goes before a fall. As St. Catherine of Genoa so wisely put it: "Renewal without reform is the corruption of the Church." Reform begins and ends with the recognition that pride is the greatest enemy within. It must be defeated daily by protracted prayer, faithful obedience and true humility.

Chapter Six

Humility, a Biblical Virtue

Someday a future Pope will have to write an encyclical letter entitled something like "Humility, a necessary way to salvation" because very limited audiences within the Church know what humility is and how to grow in it. Thomists in general have been skittish on the subject because they find it easier to argue about the nature of being or virtue in general, and sometimes neglect to write about particular virtues. "High" morality (from above) seems to be a preference to "low" morality (from below) as a subject for some reflective Thomists.

In Plato and Plutarch, the word "humility" suggests someone held in low esteem by self and others, a sense of feeling lowly or depreciated, a sign of weakness. In the Old Testament and the example of Christ however humility "combines the ideas of poverty, modesty and mildness."[1] Spicq gives a profile of the humble: little people, unfortunate sufferers, discreet and self-effacing and reserved within their community.[2] As we shall see, humility will be a cause which one opens up to God and seems to open God's heart to individual souls.

If we look at St. Thomas, especially in the *Summa Theologiae*, we find a further ramification of the scriptural data on the subject. But like many other concepts in the thought of Aquinas however, we must see humility in comparison or contrast with

---

[1] Ceslaus Spicq, O.P., James D. Ernest (ed. and trans.), *Theological Lexicon of the New Testament* (Peabody, MA: Hendrickson Publ., 1996), p. 370.

[2] Ibid., pp. 370-71.

other virtues. We need to understand something of the virtue of magnanimity and the vice of pride in order to get a firm grasp of the depth and breadth of humility.

What Is the Problem?

When theologically illiterate people hear the word "humility" preached to or at them, they are inclined to think that it is a quality of never speaking about oneself, feeling inferior, never admitting one's successes (or anyone else's for that matter), keeping oneself (and sometimes more importantly others) effaced through cutting or critical speech. Moreover, for some, the truly humble wife or religious or priest becomes the doormat to everyone and must never "talk back" or defend himself in the face of criticism or accusations. The humble person never asks for anything and is satisfied with whatever is given. Likewise, humble persons never seek to aim for higher goals in prayer or whatever. To aim for a particular better job, or promotion, or something more excellent is an attempt to do things beyond one's abilities, and this is pride. The humble person constantly suppresses the "self" in favor of the common good and the wishes of others, and always relies on God to solve his problems. And if the problems do not go away, then the humble person suffers them because he or she knows that they deserve far more sufferings for their sins than they are currently receiving.

St. Thomas knew of these false attitudes of humility and refuted them in his *Summa*.

First, it is not against humility for someone to aim at high actions worthy of praise. For Thomas, this is a possible virtue, given one's motives and personal vocation. He calls it "magnanimity" a word that goes back to Aristotle. As we saw in the previous chapter, he says: "Magnanimity by definition implies a certain aspiration of the spirit to great things" (ST II-II 129, 1). But an act can be called great both proportionately and absolutely. Simple acts can be magnanimous "when a person puts this to the best use" such as fulfilling simple responsibilities. And doing something objectively ordinary if put to best use (the glory of God, for example) can be the same virtue in ordinary persons as leading a country or army or building a skyscraper by more gifted persons. In his response to the third objection that one should run away from actions which win praise and recognition, he brilliantly says: "People are praiseworthy when they despise recognition by refusing to act meanly to gain it, and when they do not esteem it too highly. But it would be deplorable if they despised recognition by not bothering to perform acts worthy of it. In this way magnanimity is concerned with recognition, in that it is eager to do actions worthy of it, but not so as to overvalue recognition by men." So, to do great acts worthy of praise and at the same time esteeming human praise moderately is virtuous. In II-II 129, 2 ad 3, he will develop this thought even further: "for virtue which merits recognition by God cannot be sufficiently recognized by man."

Second, in comparing magnanimity to humility as virtues, Thomas, in an answer which seems to give a hint of his personality, clearly indicates how they interact with one's life:

> In man there is a quality of greatness possessed by God's gift, and a characteristic defect which comes from the weakness of his nature. Magnanimity therefore makes a man esteem himself worthy of great things through contemplating the gifts which he has from God. For example, if he has great virtue of mind, magnanimity makes him strive for attaining perfection in virtuous works; and similarly in the employment of any other good, such as knowledge or fortunate circumstances. But humility makes a man belittle himself by contemplating his own particular weakness (ST II-II 129, 3 ad 4).

He goes on to say that both virtues, magnanimity and humility are not really contradictory even "though they seem to incline to opposite directions because they have different purposes in mind." One notices right away that both virtues need the intellect as a condition for growing in the respective actualities.

Finally, Thomas sees that magnanimity is allied with courage because it strengthens the soul for a difficult task (129, 5) and develops confidence to hope of achieving something difficult (129, 6), which produces a certain freedom from undue anxiety (129, 7). And not being negative about the goods of fortune as some spiritual authors would be, Thomas concludes:

> Likewise the blessings of fortune serve as useful instruments for acts of virtue, for by the help of riches, power and friends the opportunity of achievement is presented to us. So, it is clear that the blessings of fortune contribute to magnanimity (II-II 129, 8).

What About Pride?

It is very clear from the above that problems can emerge when trying to be magnanimous in one's life: excessive search for fame and honor thereby committing the sin of ambition (ST II-II 131, 1 & 2), relying on one's self in taking on something beyond one's powers to the extent of not seeking God's help thereby committing the sin of presumption (II-II 130, 1 & 2), seeking personal glory or display of one's virtues to others in doing virtuous deeds like giving away money so that others know about it rather than seeking God's glory, thereby committing the sin of vainglory (II-II 132, 1-5). However, one can also sin by going in the opposite direction. This is called "pusillanimity":

> Everything opposed to natural inclination is a sin because it goes against the law of nature. There is, however, in everything a natural tendency to undertake action commensurate with its capability. This is evident in all natural things, whether animate or other-

wise. But just as presumption leads someone to exceed his capability by straining after what is greater than he can reach, so pusillanimity causes a man to fall short of his capability when he refuses to extend himself to achieve an aim commensurate with his powers (ST II-II 133, 1).

Pride's Hint of Magnanimity

Now, when it comes to the vice of pride, it will look similar to magnanimity for when it governs a person, he or she "craves excellence out of reason" (ST II-II 162, 1 ad 2) or for one's own superiority (162, 2). Augustine remarks (cited in the same place of the *Summa*) that, as a consequence, the proud person is a "bad imitation of God, for he hates being equal with his fellows under God, but wills to dominate them as taking God's place" (a perennial temptation of those who exercise authority). This can affect one's intellectual life for "by hugging their own excellence, the proud grow bored with the excellence of the truth itself" and they "submit their minds to learn from no one" (162, 3 ad 1). Moreover, whatever contributes to their exaggerated esteem of themselves effectively puts them into the pull of pride. Thus, the proud person dwells on other peoples' failings rather than their virtues (162, 4 ad 2).

Thomas quotes and later affirms Gregory's list of the kinds of pride:

> Gregory considered that the swelling of arrogance was displayed by four notes; *first, when people esteem their goodness as being from themselves*; second, though they believe it comes from above, they reckon they deserve it; third, they boast of qualities they do not possess; and fourth, despise others and preen themselves on the exclusive possession of the good qualities they have (ST II-II 162, 1 obj. 1).

Thomas notes in the main body of the text that while superiority results from the possession of a good, it is easy for the proud person to think he possesses more worth than he actually has. Worse still, however, is that proud people do not want to be submissive to God so that the vice "spurns the condition appointed for him by divine rule or mission, in defiance of the lesson of St. Paul: *But we will not glory beyond our measure, according to the measure of the rule which God has measured for us.*" Continuing from a religious perspective, Aquinas goes on to say that "the root of pride" is "somehow not being subject to God and his rule." God's rule, of course, means keeping his commandments as taught by the Church. When someone says that no Pope is going to tell him what he can or cannot do in the bedroom, objectively what he is "doing" is acting out of pride not simply out of lust.

In 162, 6, Aquinas shows that pride is like all sins, namely a turning against God because someone "wills not to be subject to him and his rule," and so, a turning toward creaturely goods *in an unreasonable manner.* However, some sins flow not so much from pride as from weakness and ignorance. If a person is filled with a deep seated vice of pride, sometimes God, who loves everyone, will permit these types of persons to "tumble into other sins" (carnal ones he mentions earlier) "in order to remedy it" (II-II 162, 6 ad 3).

From these aspects, it should be easy to understand how some of the angels and Adam and Eve fell from grace: they both desired some good of excellence beyond due measure and refused to depend upon God for the gifts and goods that he wanted to bestow upon them, no more and no less. St. Thomas proceeds to develop the two treatises on "the fall" based upon his analysis of pride, which seems to correspond to experience, although the Church has never officially taught anything on the subject in a formal way except to use the word (see CCC 1866), leaving its analysis to her theologians, doctors and saints.

How Does Humility Fit In?

St. Thomas is undoubtedly original in his contribution to the question of humility because, for the most part, spiritual authors gave a certain precedence to the intellect as the source and cause of humility, as some false understandings of it were explained above.

In *Summa Theologiae* II-II 161, 1 Thomas examines this *near* theological virtue since it clears the obstacles to attaining faith, hope and charity. But humility is not a theological virtue. Aquinas teaches that it is an allied virtue to temperance because it has "to temper and restrain the soul lest it press forward immoderately to high things (excelsa)." But he wisely reminds his students that magnanimity "stiffen[s] the spirit against hopelessness and hearten[s] it in the pursuit of great things in accordance with right reason...." In fact, as he said earlier, the two virtues are not in competition, but actually need each other in order to imitate Christ. On the one hand, people have gifts from God that need to be developed and actualized, on the other hand, people need to be tempered lest they go and try to excel beyond their talents and gifts.

In II-II 161, 2, Thomas shows why humility is a matter of the will but not without the intellect's help. He suggests that past theologians thought that, as pride is a matter of exaggerated self-esteem, a problem of the mind, humility must therefore be the opposite, straightening out the mind. However, Aquinas asserts that "it is necessary that he should recognize where his abilities fail to match that which surpasses them." This means that "the knowledge of one's own deficiency is a criterion of humility as a rule and criterion moderating one's appetite" (for doing great things is understood in this context). But one must actually *choose* to do this moderating and so this is a "motion of the appetite" (another name for the will).

Does this mean that one should not aim for great works? Thomas replies: "To strive after ambitious objects is contrary to humility when it issues from confidence in your own abilities, not from confidence in divine help, especially since the more one humbles oneself before God the more one is lifted up before him" (II-II 161, 2 ad 2). This pithy sentence shows how important it is that humility join up with the virtue of prayer, which begs from God the gifts to be able to accomplish his will.

He goes on to say:

> Humility essentially lies in the appetite (the will), and restrains its inordinate urge for things which are above us. Yet its rule lies in cognition, namely in a judgment not reckoning ourselves to be above what we are. The principle and root of both is the reverence we bear towards God (II-II 161, 12).

Throughout the body of this article, Thomas lists how humility influences the will, for example, by not following one's own unreasonable will and acting according to a superior's reasonable decisions, keeping to one's clearly outlined responsibilities notwithstanding hardships and difficulties. From the point of view of the intellect, the human person recognizes and acknowledges shortcomings, incapable of certain great things even to putting others above self, and how all this influences spoken demeanor, and even the stopping of senseless or silly mirth.

Humility in Relationship with Other People

The Angelic Doctor poses a serious but practical question in II-II 161, 4 that has ramifications for the workplace of the priest as well as marriage and family life, namely: should a man or woman (*homo*) submit himself to everybody out of humility? The reason for the question is that humility seems to speak to a posture of the self with regard to God and not to neighbor. Thomas says that even human beings can be evaluated according to what they have from God, for humility implies "reverence which bows down before God." While we do not have to rank ourselves greater sinners than anyone else, nor claim the gifts which we have from God less than they are, Thomas reminds us that "nevertheless you do well to admit that your neighbor has good qualities which you yourself lack, and that you have defects he does not have, and in humility to submit yourself accordingly." In II-II 161, 4 ad 2, Aquinas goes further and says we should follow Paul's advice to "*esteem others better than yourselves...*" by thinking quite sincerely there can be hidden worth in another greater than ours, even though we display a worth greater than his. How often many marriages could be saved if each of the spouses could even consider what is superior in the other as a gift from God to the other person, rather than as a threat to marital and family unity. Even children have gifts from God that parents will lack, for no one possesses the fullness of talents, gifts or virtues.

Humility as "a" Foundation for the Spiritual Life

In his question of the relative value or importance of humility, Aquinas asks in II-II 161, 5 whether humility is the sovereign virtue. His answer is quite intriguing for he states that humility as the foundation of all the virtues would seem therefore to be the greatest among them. He refutes this idea in the following manner:

> As the integration of the virtues is likened to a building, so that which is the start of gaining virtue is likened to the foundation which is laid first. Now the Christian virtues are shed on us by God. Among them coming first can be understood in a double sense. First by way of removing obstacles, and so humility holds the initial place in that it expels pride, which God resists, and makes a man submissive and ready to receive divine favor: *God resists the proud, and giveth grace to the humble* (Jm 4:6). It is in this sense that humility is said to be the foundation of the spiritual

edifice. But in another sense, directly first among the virtues is that which gives us access to God. This is faith: *He that cometh to God must believe* (Heb 11:6). In this sense faith is the nobler foundation than humility (ST II-II 161, 5 ad 2).

What is interesting in this section is that Thomas considers the spiritual life in the lived order to have not one but two foundations, humility and faith, the latter being superior since it is a theological virtue giving us immediate access to God's mind. Faith being the door which opens up the mind of God for us becomes the motivation of humility, but humility influences faith in that it puts aside one's own self-love of intellectual excellence and docilely takes in the revealed Word of God. Aquinas points out the paradox:

> Why Christ chiefly proposed humility to us is that it especially removes the obstacles to our spiritual welfare, which lies in our striving for spiritual and heavenly things, from which we are held back by preoccupation with earthly greatness. And therefore our Lord, dismissing the obstacle, showed how exterior greatness is to be scorned by his example of humility. So humility, as it were, disposes to man's free access to spiritual and divine blessings. Yes, as a perfection is better than a disposition to it, so charity and the other virtues which move directly into God's company are nobler and more potent than humility (II-II 161, 5 ad 4).

Thomas is careful to say "as it were" when speaking of humility as "disposing to spiritual and divine blessings" because he knows that the movement of the Holy Spirit and divine grace together is the cause of justification. However, Aquinas does not want to eliminate human cooperation, even though it is overshadowed by grace itself.

Conclusion

When the theologian looks at the distortions of the virtue of humility as sometimes popularly presented, and then turns to what Aquinas has accomplished in expanding the biblical notions, it is clear that humility is essential for one's salvation and necessary for sheer sanity. In the *Catechism of the Catholic Church*, we discover what humility can do when it is real: "[H]umility is the foundation of prayer. Only when we humbly acknowledge that 'we do not know how to pray as we ought,' are we ready to receive freely the gift of prayer. Man is a beggar before God" (2559). But is not prayer the task of the priest, which he cannot do very well unless he learns to live this virtue of humility?

Chapter Seven

Vainglory: Problems of Praise in the Priesthood

Before looking at the vice of vainglory which can undermine the life of a priest, a few thoughts are necessary about the notion of honor and praise so that we can more easily proceed to the analysis of the vice of vainglory as seen through the light of Aquinas.

In the very early stages of life, children need affirmation from their parents. Both fetuses and babies need to feel their goodness by the affectionate love of their parents, which takes place both in the womb and outside the womb by loving touches from father and mother. As babies mature into children, they continue to need their personal goodness affirmed from the loving words and touches of their parents and siblings. All of these actions from breast feeding to playing with the child leads the child to trust his or her mother and father so that when the parents want to give their child education in religion, morals and other cultural values, he or she will trust the parents more than television and other pop culture heroes. Furthermore as children's gifts or talents, sins and imperfections emerge, parents will help in correcting them, and at the same time help them grow in virtue and develop a sense of honesty about the limitations of their gifts. At a certain point, parents and the extended family should lead the child to discover his or her particular vocation in the plan of God.

Loving affirmation for children occurs on the level of conversing, giving praise and honor when they do well, as well as correction when they are disobedient. It can also be shown by actions, such as affectionate gestures or angry words when appropriate and necessary. Later in life, as young adults, children will hopefully honor their parents from time to time by giving them gifts out of pure generosity, thanking them, phoning or writing letters and e-mails of appreciation and affection. Other times, they will praise their parents for all the benefits which were showered upon them, and perhaps even take care of them in old age. Honoring someone is usually an act of virtue on the part of the one honoring, unless hypocrisy or other agendas are the motivation. Normally, to be honored is a reminder that one has certain virtues and gifts, and it is given as encouragement to continue growing in deeds of virtue. Many people, however, who have not received loving affirmation begin to desire honor for its own sake, or for other improper reasons. As Thomas puts it: "…for a man to desire his good to be known by someone is not properly a desire for perfection. Hence he has a certain vanity unless this is useful for some end" (*De Malo* 9, 1).

What Precisely is Vainglory?

In the *Summa Theologiae*, Thomas first analyzes the word "glory" which is "the good of a person coming to the notice and approval of many people" (ST II-II 132, 1). He goes on to say that the notice and approval can also come from a few people, a single person, or even "by oneself alone." This recognition and approval as such, even by one's very self is "not a sin" (Ibid.). Rather, the sin comes when it is vain. Before analyzing when glory is vain, it is necessary to see more of what he means by honor.

In the treatment of *dulia* or honor, sometimes translated as respectful service, St. Thomas has the following to say:

To honor means to attest to someone's superiority. Thus, as Aristotle shows, people seeking honor are looking for a testimony of their personal worth. Now there is one kind of witness to truth before God and another before men. Since God is the searcher of hearts, it is possible to honor God simply interiorly, for example by meditating on his eminence or even on the godliness of another person (ST II-II 103, 1).

Where, however, it is a question of giving testimony before men, there has to be some outward token: words, when we praise the merits of another; actions, such as bows, salutations, etc.; even objects, as when presentations are made, medals struck, etc. This is the sense in which honor consists in externals (Ibid.).

Certain questions need to be asked at this point: When is the desire for glory vain and sinful and when is it not? or, When is it reasonable and when is it disordered or unreasonable?

In the *Summa Theologiae*, Aquinas poses the question whether the *"desire for glory is a sin?"* (II-II 132, 1). Many spiritual authors would say yes; Thomas says no with some qualifications for the following reasons:

But the recognition and approval of one's own good is not a sin. In St. Paul's words, *We have received not the spirit of the world, but the Spirit which is from God, that we might understand the gifts bestowed on us by God.* Likewise, it is not a sin to desire the approval of others for one's good deeds, for in *Matthew* we read *Let your light shine before men.* So desire for glory in itself does not denote anything sinful. But a desire for empty or vain glory does denote a fault, for it is sinful to seek any vain thing. As the *Psalm* says, *How long will you love vain words, and seek after lies?* (II-II 132, 1).

"...praise and honorable recognition are related to glory as causes from which glory proceeds. So glory is related to them as their end. It is because of glory that a person loves recognition and praise, since he believes that through it he will have renown in the sight of others (II-II 132, 4 ad 2).

He says glory is vain and enters into a person's character in a disordered way when he "seeks glory for a non-existent thing, or an object unworthy of glory," or seeks glory from someone who is of "unsound judgment" but above all when a person "does not apply his desire for it to a proper end such as God's honor or his neighbor's edification" (ST II-II 131, 2). Thomas further nuances his meaning when he says:

> Perfection entails self-knowledge, but a man does not need to be known by others to achieve perfection, and so he ought not to seek such fame for its own sake. Yet it can be sought insofar as it has a useful purpose. This may be the glorification of God by men, or improvement in men as a result of the good which they recognize in another; or a man may recognize his own good qualities as a result of the laudatory testimony of others, and therefore eagerly persist in them and advance to higher things. In this sense it is praiseworthy to be careful of one's good name and to take thought for what is noble in the sight of men; but not to take empty pleasure in the praise of men (II-II 131, 2 ad 3).

But if there is utility in being honored by someone, what is it? Thomas gives three reasons for seeking human glory and praise:

> First to the glory of God, by someone's good being manifested glory is given to God to whom as its primary author that good is principally attributed; hence it is said in Matthew (5:16), "Even so let your light shine before men, in order that they may see your good works and give glory to your Father in heaven." Secondly, it is useful for the salvation of our neigh-

bors, who seeing a person's goodness, are motivated to imitate him, according to 1 Corinthians 10, "let each one of you please his neighbor by doing good for his edification." In a third way glory can be ordered to the profit of the man himself who, when he considers that his good works are praised by others gives thanks because of them and persists in them more firmly; hence the Apostle frequently recalls to the mind of the faithful in Christ their good works so that they may more firmly persist in them (*De Malo* 9, 1).

Still further, in the question concerning the causes of happiness or beatitude where he is looking for that which brings about our ultimate fulfillment, St. Thomas asks whether it can be found in fame or glory (ST I-II 2, 4). He notes that if happiness is man's true good, it cannot be the result of something illusory such as praise which is sometimes falsely created. Neither can being well known or recognized by other people alone be the cause of happiness since recognition or pre-eminence is caused by something additional that is intrinsic to the person. Eventually in his treatment of happiness (ST I-II 1-5), he shows that from the faith perspective, the cause of total happiness is the beatific vision of the Triune God.

Thomas continues to probe the issue when he asks whether it is natural that a person wishes his good to be known by others. He has already said that the desire to be praised is not a desire for perfection. So, we would expect that the answer to this question would also be a resounding "no," for the humble person prefers to be unknown and hidden according to some schools of spirituality. But the Common Doctor again surprises us with the following answer:

Every perfect being naturally communicates itself to others so far as is possible, and this belongs to each thing in imitation of the first perfect being, namely God, who communicates his goodness to all he creates; but the good of a person is communicated to others both as regards being and as regards knowledge; **hence it seems to pertain to a natural desire that a person wishes his good to become known**. If then this is referred to the proper end, it will pertain to virtue, but if not, it will pertain to vanity (*De Malo* 9, 1 ad 3).

In another context Thomas repeats with a further distinction the notion about the natural desire for glory:

By human glory, [a man] achieves pre-eminence in human affairs. Hence because glory is closely related to pre-eminence which men desire most of all, it logically follows that it is greatly desirable and that many vices arise from a disordered desire for it. Thus vainglory is a capital sin (ST II-II 132, 4).

The difference then is quite simple: is the desire ordered or disordered? St. Thomas indicates as much also by citing the Roman author Sallust, "The virtuous strive for glory in the right way, that is, by means of virtue; and this is not to seek glory out of vanity but to strive for it in an orderly manner" (*De Malo* 9, 1 ad 7). Most fundamentally, then, the question is: When is glory-seeking really vain or disordered? Thomas answers:

...when a person glories either about something false or about something temporal or when he does not refer to his glory to its proper end" (*De Malo* 9, 2).

By something false he gives as an example when a person glories in his singing "when in fact he sings badly, or who glories because he owns a horse that runs well" (Ibid.). The latter example might today be seen in someone who wishes to be honored for owning a very expensive car. As for something temporal, vainglory might arise because someone knows a famous person and seeks the publicity of honor from others simply because of this friendship or even acquaintanceship.

The vice of vainglory can be moderately to gravely dangerous to one's salvation, because as Thomas asserts, it "easily leads to a man's eternal destruction inasmuch as it causes him to place his trust in himself; hence it is said to be a most dangerous sin not so much because of its gravity but because it is a disposition to more serious sin" (*De Malo* 9, 2 ad 4). In the *Summa Theologiae*, Aquinas says that "vainglory becomes presumptuous" and a person becomes "overconfident in himself. In this way it gradually causes him to be sapped of the good qualities within him" (ST II-II 132, 3 ad 3). The precise grave sin then could be loving "human approval... more than the observance of God's commands" (*De Malo* 9, 2 ad 9). Looking back over the past thirty years, we can think of those theologians who publicly and radically dissented from *Humanae Vitae* because they may have wanted to be popular with the people and their fellow theologians. Also, a pastor, whether priest or bishop, can fail to teach the full truth about human sexuality because he fears losing the esteem of the people who may not want to hear the correct teaching of the Church. He may also fear his collections will go down. Therefore, he might speak only about a vague love of neighbor and being merciful like the Sacred Heart of Jesus without mentioning the other "hard truths."

Other major problems that flow from vanity are its outcomes; Aquinas calls them "daughters." He uses these metaphors "mother" and "daughters" because they are conceived within itself as if a mother vice could conceive within herself without the male. She would then only produce daughters (*De Malo* 9, 3). Vanity, then, spawns disobedience, boasting, hypocrisy, contention, obstinacy, discord, and what Thomas calls presumption of novelties. If pride seeks excellence beyond one's due limits, then vainglory, one of pride's lieutenants, "strives to manifest itself and from that very manifestation seeks to gain a kind of excellence" (Ibid., 9, 3 ad 1). This is also why Thomas teaches that "all the daughters of vainglory have an affinity with pride" (Ibid.). He writes:

> Now a man can manifest his own excellence in two ways: in one way directly, and in another way, indirectly. Directly either by words and such is boasting; or by deeds that are genuine and an occasion of astonishment, and such is the presumption of novelties, for novel or singular deeds are usually a greater source of astonishment to men; or by deeds that are feigned and such is hypocrisy. And indirectly a man manifests his excellence by striving to show he is not inferior to another. And this in regard to four things: first, as regards the intellect, and such is obstinacy, by which a man relying on his own judgment is unwilling to accept a sounder judgment; secondly, as regards the will, and such is discord, when a man refuses to concur with the will of better men; thirdly, as regards discourse, and such is contention, when a man is unwilling to be outdone in a discussion or argument with another; fourthly, as regards deeds, when someone is unwilling to subject his actions to the command of a superior and this is disobedience (*De Malo* 9, 4).

When applying the Preferred Doctor's teaching to the clergy, we can easily see how this vice of vainglory can undermine one's spiritual life. First of all clerics need a good reputation to effectively exercise the task of governing the lay people of God appropriate to their rank. One of the reasons why some clergy of all ranks need to be removed from their responsibilities from time to time is that they no longer generate trust among the people. Thomas is very insightful in this regard when he writes about the evil of detraction:

> It is a serious thing to take away another's reputation, for a man's reputation is one of his most precious tem-

poral possessions and he is prevented from doing many good deeds if it is damaged. This is why *Sirach* says, *Have regard to your name, since it will remain for you longer than a thousand great stores of gold*. Detraction as such, therefore is a mortal sin (ST II-II 73, 2).

Additionally, Thomas states that the clergy deserve respect (or what is often called "observance") for their office which is a kind of honor:

> When a person is in a position of authority, he has not only eminence of rank but also some particular power to rule over those subject to him. It is as one who governs others, then, that he stands as a giver of life. Endowments of learning or virtue on the other hand do not give a person this distinction but simply go to make up personal worth. This is why there is a special virtue bent upon offering honor and homage only to those in authority. Still it is true that one becomes fit for a position of rank through learning, virtue and the like; so the deference which is shown to others because of superiority of any sort engages this same virtue (ST II-II 105, 1 ad 2).

While it normally happens that clergy experience such honor, praise or deference, given to their persons because of the office they possess, they must also earn some of it personally by fidelity to their responsibilities as preachers, teachers and through a prudent sense of governance. Clerics possessing supernatural authority from God "have a right to honor, which means in fact the acknowledgment of another's eminence" (II-II 105, 3). Also, Aquinas in the same article makes note that the right to homage includes obedience to one's commands and recompense in reasonable measure.

Now, with such a rank in the Church, the priest, deacon or bishop is open to all kinds of temptations to seek glory badly and not in due order. Being in charge of a diocese or a CCD office can lead one to feel he is doing a great job and needs to be given an unreasonable amount of adulation. He can begin to act with such a mean spirit that his approach will be motivated by a personal desire for glory as a minor or major end in itself, and not for the good of the people under him. He may begin with the small desire for recognition for his talents and ultimately be consumed by the desire to be seen as most outstanding. When he does not receive this degree of recognition, he will retaliate against his subordinates, criticizing them as a means to boost his own self-esteem.

As we saw above, the problem of vainglory leads to the daughter vices namely, disobedience, boasting, hypocrisy, contention, obstinacy, discord, presumption, novelties.

Beginning with the last vice, it is evident that liturgical abuses are frequently perpetrated so that some clergy can feel admired for their creativity and receive attention from both their flocks and from other clergy as being "progressive." He thinks that riding up the aisle of the church on a donkey or in a Volkswagen on Palm Sunday, or doing a amateurish dance on Easter will bring some kind of favorable fame. Or, he builds a new church building that to all appearances seems outrageous in its ability to flaunt the rules of sacred architecture as a monument of honor to himself.

Disobedience is perhaps the most harmful way of showing the spirit of vainglory since it attacks the virtue of religion and weakens faith since it hardens one's spirit to surrender to God's will as manifested in legitimate authority. Thomas understands well this problem:

> Vainglory craves to show off some form of superiority; because to refuse to submit to another's commands gives the impression of adding to one's own superiority, disobedience does arise from vainglory (ST II-II 105, 1 ad 2).

The great temptation to become one's own lawmaker over and against the laws of the Church as found in the *Code of Canon Law* and elsewhere looms large when clergy possess some limited authority. Some, rather than accepting the limits of their office, strive to go beyond them. Occasionally when a pastor proceeds to conduct a marriage ceremony for people with diriment impediments, he believes he himself can adjudicate marriage cases and by his own alleged or usurped authority dispense with what he sees as the "legalism" of the law or its lack of mercy. Pastors sometimes do similar things when they grant general absolution for their parish apart from the authority of the bishop of the diocese or attempt to provide internal forum solutions for "failed" marriages without the due process of canon law.

Boasting about one's various achievements as if they were not modest but nearly heroic is another way of drawing attention to oneself because it exaggerates any good actually done, and forgets that all good works are primarily done by God as the primary cause. This is the case of a bishop in a small diocese who each month writes up reports concerning his diocese to members of the Roman curia in order to keep his name on their minds so that some day he might receive the gift of a more prestigious diocese. Or, there may exist cases of bishops whose Catholic newspaper always touts throughout the year the story of their good works with many pictures of their smiling faces to prove it. Finally, and quite often, one of the great temptations of bishops is to go over the heads of their priests and seek the advice and presence of the more wealthy laity, especially enjoying their compliments when they follows their advice. As a result, they have more reason to boast to other bishops and priests.

The problem with hypocrisy is more complex and somewhat worse as a vice flowing from vainglory according to St. Thomas:

> There are two factors in hypocrisy, namely the absence of holiness, and the pretence of its presence. If by a hypocrite we mean one whose intention is

marked by a duplicity of having no regard for holiness while merely appearing to be holy — the usual usage in Scripture — then it is clearly a mortal sin. No one is totally lacking in holiness except by reason of mortal sin.

If, however, we take a hypocrite to be one who intends to feign the holiness he lacks because of mortal sin, then, even though he is in a state of mortal sin and so wanting in holiness, the deception itself is not always a mortal sin, but at times a venial sin.

We should judge which of the two it is by the end involved. When it is incompatible with charity towards God or neighbor, the sin will be mortal — when **for example if he puts on the guise of holiness in order to spread false teaching, or to gain some ecclesiastical rank, of which he is unworthy, or any temporal advantage one which he settles as his final end.**

When the end intended is not contrary to charity, the sin will be venial — for example when someone simply finds delight in deceiving; of such a person Aristotle says that *he seems empty-headed rather than wicked.* The same criterion applies to deception as to lying (ST II-II 111, 4).

Sometimes, it is possible that a small number of clerics may pretend to have special degrees or awards which do not exist, and show them off in order to curry favor with civil authorities or the people. This is the outright but hidden spreading of a false reputation.

Contention and obstinacy are very much related to each other. The former is based upon the false idea that one is more intelligent than another person and so he stubbornly sticks to his opinion. He does not discuss and make distinctions, but rather argues his positions because they are his reasons. So, in parish council meetings, finance meetings, Father or Bishop is always right and cannot take in the truth or its practical nuances, nor distinguish facts from fiction, because he has to be the sole author of the truth in his projects. Obstinacy, on the other hand, deals with the problem of holding "overmuch to his own opinion because he wishes by doing so to show off his own excellence; so obstinacy springs from vainglory as its cause" (ST II-II 138, 2 ad 1). In the *Commentary on Aristotle's Nicomachean Ethics*, Thomas defines the word:

> The word obstinacy refers to the headstrong, since these people are both undisciplined and rude. Opinionated by pleasure and pain, they are glad to win an argument and to remain convinced in their opinion. But they grieve if their judgments seem weak and only opinions. Therefore they bear more resemblance to the incontinent than the continent man.[1]

Throughout the *Summa* and here in the *De Malo*, St. Thomas will refer to heretics as obstinate people who prefer their own opinions to the revelation of God:

> Heresy implies obstinacy which alone gives rise to a heretic while obstinacy arises from pride, for it is a sign of great pride that a person prefer his own opinion to divinely revealed truth (*De Malo* 8, 1 ad 7).

In other contexts, certain sinners as the bad angels and people in hell are called obstinate because they are filled with malice. Also, it is considered a specific sin against the Holy Spirit as well. But in the context of vainglory, it is something else, that stubbornness which may also motivate contention in words.

Finally, discord means a failure to join in the single or common will of others in pursuing a project. This can especially be

---

[1] Thomas Aquinas, *Commentary on Aristotle's Nicomachean Ethics*, C.I. Litzinger, tr. (Chicago: Regnery, 1964), Bk. 7, Lect. 9, 1444.

the case when the majority of good men vote to do an action, and someone holds back his vote or consent or votes against the issue for reasons other than his unwillingness to cooperate. This is frequently because he did not think of the idea in the first place or has his own ideas turned down by the majority. It is a clash of wills that he feels demeans his honor.

It becomes evident that the solution to the problem of vainglory, like pride itself, is humility or an attitude that realizes there are limits to one's gifts, accomplishments and ideas. But faith also needs to guide one so that he does not believe he is the primary cause of holiness in others and that God deserves the honor, praise, and glory far exceeding what any of us can deserve from others in the sacred ministry. To live this way, requires fidelity to deep meditation and contemplation with large doses of examination of conscience so that each will know his place in the continuum of doing, not his apostolate, but Christ's. In this instance, success in one's ministerial life can be the loss of one's soul, especially when looked upon as an end in itself. For instead of seeking the glory of God and the salvation of souls, the priest seeks himself and spreads his own kingdom of glory, honor and praise.

Chapter Eight

The Desire for the Episcopate and the Sin of Ambition

The Question of Promotion

One very small issue that could have been considered, but was not, is whether it is reasonable for a seminarian or priest to want to be a member of the College of Bishops and whether he should actively campaign for this "better work." In the world of the secular workplace, it is reasonable for lay members of the Christian faithful to want promotions and higher positions within a company so that they may help the company produce better goods and services for the common good, achieve more profits, and help their families prosper. No one doubts for a moment that this is a good aspiration, unless motivated from unreasonable desires, such as covetousness or avarice, envy and vainglory. However, it is also the case that great moral virtue is not normally required for assuming leadership roles in corporations because they were not founded as institutes for pursuing perfection of the spiritual life or "saving souls." Yet is the priesthood of itself a lower stage that looks to something higher similar to a promotion? Moreover, is it reasonable for a bishop, either an auxiliary or a diocesan bishop, to long for a diocese or a better one that will give him a higher title and more responsibilities, if not the red hat or even white zuchetto itself?

As we shall see, St. Thomas Aquinas has some valuable insights on these questions which could produce better bishops for the people of God, if the present College of Bishops with the Pope officially adopted at least some of his positions. While it would make it more difficult for the Holy See to find suitable candidates if the Thomistic principles are held onto with firmness, overall, better men will be chosen as a result.

A Challenge Is Posed

Several months ago, a retired Cardinal began a small campaign against bishops who seek to become archbishops to obtain "better sees." It was Cardinal Gantin who opined that once in office, a bishop should remain there for the duration as was the case from the earliest times, assuming of course the right of the Pope to make other provisions according to his determination. Somehow, according to the Cardinal, desiring or aspiring and actively campaigning to do more and seek "higher things" with a higher place or rank within the episcopate itself is unbecoming for someone already a bishop since his ring signifies that he is married to his diocese. But is it also unbecoming for a priest to want to become a bishop if he is convinced that the Church really needs his expertise? Once a priest or bishop feels he has a call from God to go higher, must he actively pursue it?

Many years ago, I met the then only Trappist bishop in the world. He had been in Rome doing some business for his community. Shortly after arriving, he was called to one of the offices of the Roman Curia and told that he was to become a bishop in his native land. He asked if he had any choice in the matter and the reply was given: "With diocesan priests we ask, but with religious we tell." He became somewhat downcast for several months over losing his life of contemplation, but eventually overcame that difficulty because he was vowed to obedience and the requisites of its new circumstances.

Actively Lobbying for Promotion

Occasionally, one hears it said among priests that only a fool would want to be a bishop during these turbulent times because of the grave difficulties encountered in the modern Church and society. Yet, at the same time, it becomes evident that small clusters of priests (and bishops) band together in the hopes that a few of them, at least, will achieve higher offices within the Church because of their discrete (and sometimes not so discrete) lobbying. They feel a special love for the Church and they think they have the solutions. Sadly, it is frequently the fact that once they achieve their objective, many do not seem to understand what the Christian faithful's real needs are. They have so concentrated their minds and hearts on obtaining higher office or rank that they have neglected seeking the knowledge of divine truth about God's inner being and human nature from God's perspective. Also, it appears that some want to be loved, esteemed and praised by their flocks and their fellow priests rather than to lead them. In other words, the active hunger and search (St. Thomas Aquinas will call this, only when sinful, "coveting" or "avarice" either for a higher office or for the miter and crozier) causes more problems than solutions. Although the office of bishop or archbishop might be successfully achieved, this seems to lead some men to an interior blindness to spiritual realities. Consequently, this fixation of one's desire for better offices seems to diminish both the deeper thirst for the divine truth upon which the salvation of souls depends, and the strength to endure criticism for future manifest mistakes and negligence. This blindness follows naturally and easily from any excessive desire for material or created goods. As Aquinas states in his treatment on prudence and solicitude about created things:

> ... solicitude about temporal things may be unlawful through too much earnestness in endeavoring to obtain temporal things, the result being that a man is drawn away from spiritual things which ought to be

the chief object of his search, wherefore it is written (Mt 13:22) that "the care of this world... chokes up the word." Thirdly, through over much fear, when, to wit, a man fears to lack necessary things if he do what he ought to do. Now our Lord gives three motives for laying aside this fear. First, on account of the yet greater favors bestowed by God on man, independently of his solicitude, viz., his body and soul (Mt 6:26); secondly, on account of the care with which God watches over animals and plants without the assistance of man, according to the requirements of their nature; thirdly, because of Divine providence, through ignorance of which the gentiles are solicitous in seeking temporal goods before all others. Consequently He concludes that we should be solicitous most of all about spiritual goods, hoping that temporal goods also may be granted us according to our needs, if we do what we ought to do (ST II-II 55, 6).

Ecclesiastical Office as Related to Avarice

At first it might seem that being a bishop or possessing a higher office which puts one in charge of others is not a temporal thing. In an earlier work, Thomas had this to say about the material side of the office of bishop:

> St. Gregory says in his Pastoral, "that the truly praiseworthy condition under which to accept a bishopric, would be, if a man were to know as a certainty, that such an office would involve severe torture." Again, he says, "It is not every man who loves the sanctity of the episcopal office. But that sanctity is completely ignored by those, who, aspiring to such a dignity, are entranced by the idea of having others subject to them, are rejoiced at the thought of being praised, set

their hearts on being honored, and rejoice at the prospect of affluence. In such a case as that, men are coveting worldly advancement under the disguise of an office, in which it is their duty to try to extirpate earthly ambition."[1]

Even though higher ecclesiastical offices are spiritual realities, the temporal honors and glory connected with them can be very attractive as ends for themselves, and so can easily override the spiritual dimension or responsibilities of the office, as Thomas will affirm (cf. ST II-II 185, 1). But how can the desire for the episcopacy lead to such blindness, since it is a special ordination or consecration to be received with all the graces attached to this fullness of orders? If someone is looking for growth in grace and wisdom, is the episcopal office not a spiritual entity and so to be desired?

Possible Sins Committed When Seeking Office

St. Thomas Aquinas speaks somewhat of this problem in several places of his writings, especially in the *Summa Theologiae*. Thomas in his wisdom reflects on this problem in his treatment of the sin of ambition and its relationship to other vices. Additionally, Aquinas writes of the spirit of covetousness or avarice that seeks higher rank above others in the Church and this may cause a host of other problems because it is usually unreasonable (cf. ST II-II 185, 1 & 2).

In ST II-II 185, 1, Thomas poses the question: is it lawful to want the episcopate? The first two objections raise the issues posed by St. Paul seeming to say without qualification that to desire the episcopacy is to desire a good work and so is lawful

---

[1] Thomas Aquinas, *The Religious State, The Episcopate and the Priestly Office*, John Proctor, O.P., tr. (Westminster, MD: The Newman Press, 1950), p. 108.

and praiseworthy. Of the two objections, the second one is more remote or abstract in our times. It states, then: if it is good to enter the religious state of perfection, then (since the state of bishops is more perfect than that of religious) it must logically be praiseworthy to desire to be promoted to the office of bishop, since one would also be in the state of perfection!

In the sed contra, Aquinas simply quotes without comment St. Augustine who says that to be a bishop is "unbecomingly desired." In the body of the article, Thomas first states that the episcopacy means working for the good of one's fellows which also entails a higher rank over others. Moreover, the office itself deserves, as a consequence: reverence, honor, and abundance of temporal goods to get the work done. Thomas then says:

> To desire the episcopacy for the benefits connected with it is obviously unlawful and proceeds from avarice or ambition... Regarding the second element — excellency of rank — desire of the episcopacy for that reason is presumptuous (ST II-II 185, 1).

Notice in this section, there may be two distinct sins involved here, avarice (another word for covetousness) and presumption, but both are a matter of motive rather than desiring something intrinsically evil. Simply seeking the office in itself does not appear to be intrinsically evil. The next paragraph furthers this position:

> But to desire to help one's fellow man is in itself praiseworthy and virtuous. Yet since episcopal ministry carries with it a high rank, it would seem presumptuous, except in case of evident necessity, to desire this dignity in order to help one's subjects (Ibid.).

Continuing, Thomas makes the next idea his own when he quotes Gregory the Great to the effect that it would be praiseworthy to desire the episcopate when one would be certain that he would experience great suffering! This is one of the few (perhaps the only) times that Thomas, using Gregory, affirms explicitly the notion of desiring and choosing one's own cross as one consents to becoming a bishop.

The Desire for the Episcopacy Not Evil as Such

In summary, the desire to be a bishop is presumptuous if it flows from the spirit of covetousness or avarice. However, on the rare occasion of manifest or evident necessity, which elicits a desire to help others through the office, and given the particular and special necessities that will also entail carrying a cross, these can be very good motives. One could perhaps think of isolated dioceses in the world where there are no bishops or the legitimate bishop is impeded. In such places, a desire for the office could be praiseworthy, but the reader should notice that Thomas goes no further than a simple desire, as distinct from active lobbying. Thus, given the above qualifications, desiring the office of bishop is praiseworthy and, if elicited interiorly with charity, is also meritorious. This latter assertion follows from Thomas' theology of merit.

Continuing in the body of the same article, Aquinas goes on to say that a person can, without presumption, "desire" to fulfill the ministry of bishop if he is already in that office, or "desire to be worthy" of doing such a ministry, since he desires the good works of the office and not simply the dignity of rank as such. This is the very meaning of "worthy" desiring the good works of the office and not simply the dignity of rank. This article next distinguishes and separates the good from bad motives in the desire, and at the same time answers the problem raised by St. Paul's quotation in the first objection.

In answer to the second objection, Thomas wisely reasons that being in the religious state does not presuppose perfection but is "a way" to perfection. "Yet it is presumptuous to consider oneself perfect, but not for one to tend to perfection" (ST II-II 185, 1 ad 2). What Thomas means is that the episcopacy is considered to be the state of perfection and the bishop as one who is already perfected enough in virtue so as to be a perfector of others.[2] If, however, someone holds himself as already perfect, given human nature, he is not only very presumptuous but also, as Thomas will say, in another section of his writings, probably motivated by an interior act of pride. St. Thomas warns that "He who is promoted to the episcopal state is elevated to provide for others. And no one should take this promotion upon himself, according to St. Paul, 'neither does any man take the honor to himself, but he who is called by God' (Heb 5:4)" (Ibid. ad 2). This seems to show that Aquinas is against lobbying for this position, since the call is properly confirmed by higher authority to the person rather than something exclusively originating within a person.

Reading the insights of Thomas concerning the sin of presumption shows what can easily happen when one does lobby for positions of higher authority:

> Presumption is twofold; one whereby a man relies on his own power, when he attempts something beyond his power, as though it were possible to him. Such like presumption clearly arises from vainglory; for it is owing to a great desire for glory that a man attempts things beyond his power, and especially novelties which call for greater admiration. Hence Gregory states explicitly that presumption of novelties is a daughter of vainglory (ST II-II 21, 4).

---

[2]   This would not be the case with superiors in religious institutes where all including superiors are considered to be striving for perfection and so superiors need only possess a certain gift of prudence for governing.

When to Decline the Office of Bishop

In another work written earlier than the *Summa*, entitled in English *The Religious State*, Thomas draws some practical but probable conclusions about perfection and presumption in the matter of the episcopate:

> Hence, it is evident, that elevation to the episcopate assumes perfection in the person thus honored; and that it would be the height of presumption, for any man to consider himself perfect. Even St. Paul says, "Not as though I had already attained or were already perfect" (Ph 3:12). Again, in the same chapter, he adds, "Let us, therefore, as many as are perfect, be thus minded." To desire perfection, and to strive to follow after it, is not presumption. It is that holy zeal to which St. Paul exhorts us, saying, "Be ye, therefore, zealous for the better gifts" (1 Cor 12:31). Hence, it is praiseworthy to wish to embrace the religious life, although a desire for the episcopate is gross presumption. St. Gregory says, in his Pastoral, "He who has refused a bishopric has not completely resisted it; and he who has willed to be raised to it, has first seen himself cleansed by the stone of the altar." By these words we are to understand, that a man, chosen for the episcopate, should not absolutely refuse this honor. Nor yet should he aspire to it, unless he knows that he be cleansed in preparation for it. Nor should anyone, who is not thus purified, dare to approach the sacred mysteries. Neither, if he be chosen by divine grace, for this dignity, ought he, through pride disguised as humility, decline to accept it. But, as it is exceedingly difficult for any man to know whether he be purified or not, the safest course is to decline a bishopric.[3]

---

[3] *The Religious State*, p. 109.

It should be noted here how fine a route Thomas takes in saying neither a yes nor no to the question, and then comes up with a middle ground which is both a reasonable and safe conclusion.

Obedience to Higher Authority to Accept Higher Office

Returning to *Summa Theologiae* II-II 185, 2, Aquinas further refines his thought when he says: "Hence, just as it shows an inordinate will if one by his own initiative seeks to be placed in authority over others, so also it shows a disordered will if one, contrary to the command of a superior, absolutely refuses the aforesaid office of government." Here he gives a twofold distinction in the cause of persons sinning with a "disordered" will: someone who wants to be placed over others simply speaking, and runs for office as politicians do, and the contrary spirit of someone who refuses to be over others when this is against the virtue of obedience. The command of a superior today in the Latin Church as in the time of St. Thomas is the calling of the Roman Pontiff to become a bishop.

Further deepening his thought on the problem of disobedience (II-II 185, 2 ad 3), Thomas concludes by teaching that "to accept the episcopate is not of itself necessary for salvation, but it can become so because of the command of a superior...." This response would show there are sufficient reasons for refusing the office of bishop (as Aquinas and so many other saints refused this office), since it is not a sacrament necessary for salvation, except under obedience. Other than in virtue of a formal command, not only lobbying but also accepting the episcopate when not ordered to do so but simply asked by the Roman Pontiff with the right of refusal, would probably be flawed since there are already easier and more efficacious ways to salvation either for oneself or for others.

The Sin of Ambition

Now, in an earlier part of the *Summa*, II-II 131, 1 Thomas develops yet another line of thought on our problem. In the first objection, he says that ambition as such is praiseworthy because a person seeks the good of recognition or honor which is the greatest of external goods. And in the third objection, he teaches that anything helpful to the encouragement of good and discouragement of evil cannot possibly be sinful. Therefore, it is good to be ambitious for high office in the Church.

But in the sed contra, St. Paul is quoted as saying that *charity is not ambitious* (1 Cor 13:5). Within the body of the article, he further distinguishes and refines his argument:

> … recognition means a respect accorded to someone in witness of his excellence. Any human excellence raises two points. The first is that man is not the source of his own excellence; rather it is a divine gift within him, so in this sense recognition is owed chiefly to God and not to the man. Secondly, we are to realize that nothing in which a man excels is given him by God except to benefit others. So he ought to be gratified by the tribute (or testimony) which others accord to his excellence only if this tribute enables him to benefit others (ST II-II 131, 1).

The reader will notice that unlike some spiritual authors, Thomas is not afraid or negative about receiving praise from others, but is careful to understand it correctly, namely, as a way of benefitting others by personal encouragement to greater fidelity in one's work. He continues in the same paragraph about the bad consequences of a disordered longing for praise:

> The desire for recognition therefore can be unbalanced in three ways. First, a man can seek recognition of an

excellence which he does not possess; which means seeking more than one's true share of recognition. Secondly, he can desire honor for himself without acknowledgment to God. Thirdly, his desire can rest content with recognition itself, without applying it to the service of others. But ambition denotes an unbalanced desire for recognition, and so clearly it is always a sin (Ibid.).

Here he shows how honor and praise can be received sinfully in the person although he locates it in the person whose desires for it are disordered or sought in an unbalanced way and not in the "recognition" itself. Therefore, one can easily conclude that it is also flawed if a man seeks the office of bishop for these reasons.

To answer the first objection, Thomas says that the human will's desiring of any good ought to be guided by reason. Thus paradoxically, being completely indifferent to honor could be sinful if "reason commands one to seek (it) so as to avoid the evil of lack of reputation, and this is blameworthy" (my translation). For Thomas, everyone should be reasonably concerned about his or her reputation in an ordered way because a good reputation, which is a person's greatest external good, enables one to help others as it is so necessary for creating an atmosphere of trust in human relations. Thomas summarizes saying that one should "take care of one's good name but not take empty pleasure in human praise" (ST II-II 132, 1 ad 3).

Recognition or human glory is to be regarded as a reward for virtue because in the eyes of other people there is no higher way to show gratitude to the virtuous man than with recognition. The virtuous man, however, does not seek after recognition but after the true reward of one's virtue, namely beatitude or happiness.

Again, after these general considerations, the Angelic Doctor zeros in on the problem of desiring the episcopacy from another angle:

Because of the eminence of their position, recognition is due to men who are established in high office. In this sphere an unbalanced desire for high office is a characteristic of ambition. For if a person sought such office unreasonably, not for the purpose of recognition but because he aspired to a right use of it beyond his powers, he would be presumptuous rather than ambitious (ST II-II 36, 2 ad 2).

Here Thomas will only suggest, and even at that only implicitly, that seeking the office could conceivably be reasonable if not ambitious or presumptuous.

The Desire for Office as Distinguished from Seeking It

What is most interesting in all these texts cited above is that Thomas defends the "desire" for rank or episcopal office only under two conditions: if the person seeks the good of others, and if there is a special condition which seems to warrant that a particular person fill the job. This would imply that a diocesan priest might desire or aspire interiorly for episcopal office, though competent ecclesiastical authority must determine if there is a special need. It is not so clear that a religious priest should do so, since, strictly speaking, he is neither commonly ordained for a particular diocese nor for parochial ministry. Being a religious, he has to the degree laid down in law of his institute, distanced himself or "left the world" only to return to it "from the outside," as it were, as a minister of the gospel. It is for this reason that many institutes in their constitutions forbid religious to accept the episcopate unless compelled by higher authority.

So, the sin of ambition is present either wanting to be above others for its own sake, which is pride (ST II-II 162, 2 & 4), or wanting to possess public honor and esteem from others for its own sake, which is vainglory based upon presumption. However, the desire or disposition to want to suffer and love people through higher office is good and to desire the virtues necessary to be a bishop is good. Yet, it is not a good object as a consequence to seek actively or lobby directly for higher office, if for no other reason than that a priest already can do all the possible good through his prayer, his crosses and ministry, which can extend beyond his parish. It is said in the Dominican Order, and possibly other traditions as well, "The office (in this case, superiorships) seeks you; you do not seek the office."

Aquinas' More Mature Position

Thomas will makes a more definitive and nuanced position known later in another work when he teaches:

> I answer: it must be said that Augustine solves this question in *De civitate Dei*, 19, where he says that a ruling office, without which the people cannot be governed, is not fittingly sought even if it be administered as is fitting, because he who seeks a ruling office is either proud or unjust. Now it is a matter of injustice for someone to want to take more honor for himself, either power or other goods, unless he is worthy of greater things, as is said in *Ethics* 5, 3, but it is a matter of pride and presumption for someone to esteem himself to be more worthy for a ruling office than all those over whom he takes office. Hence clearly whoever seeks a ruling office is either unjust or proud. And therefore, no one ought to succeed to a ruling office by his desire, but only by God's judgment, according to what the Apostle says in Hebrews 5:4, "No one takes this honor for himself except the one who is called by God as Aaron was." But anyone is permitted to desire himself to be worthy of a rul-

ing office, or to desire the works of a good prelate for which honor is due (*Quodl.* 2, 6, 1).[4]

What is also especially striking here is the underlying notion that one can be unjust by seeking higher office, the injustice being that someone else who is truly worthy of the office is denied it!

Considerations from Spiritual Theology

If then, a man sees great needs in a diocese that require a bishop to solve the problem, the desire to be that bishop, all things considered, is good. However, Thomistic principles and the spiritual tradition would then add that there are higher and better desires which are within reach of all priests: to love penance and prayer in order to atone for sinners in a diocese or for those causing troubles within a diocese. Additionally, instead of the desire for office, one should yearn to grow in charity so that one will merit a better bishop who will lead the diocese to the heights of holiness. Moreover, if one is already a bishop, growing in charity and the virtues is more important than seeking an even higher or "better" diocese associated with more difficult works or responsibilities. For ultimately, in the spiritual life, what matters is not the amount or difficulties of the toil expended, but the depth of one's divine love done in whatever ministry flows from the priestly or episcopal office. Quite often, hidden behind a desire for authority and power over others is an escape from the true challenge of the spiritual life to expand not outwardly in diverse works, but more profoundly in deeper desires for the purity of divine love lived more directly under the gifts of the Holy Spirit than in works accomplished predominantly by reason and faith. Thomistic theologians have explained it to

---

[4] Thomas Aquinas, *Quodlibetal Questions 1 and 2*, Sandra Edwards, ed. & tr. (Toronto, Canada: Pontifical Institute of Medieval Studies, 1983).

mean living in the divine mode, rather than the human mode of virtue. Another, perhaps better expression of this good is: living the mystical way rather than the ascetical way is the summit of the journey of the spiritual life while on earth. St. John of the Cross states it differently when he says that pure love of God is worth more than a great number of works without it.

If someone loses this sense of the mystical direction of the spiritual life while wanting to grow deeper in a relationship with God, the temptation is to think that higher things means doing "more works" with higher rank,[5] campaigning for promotions, and the like rather than wanting to grow in interior divine charity and greater humility with magnanimity.

A bishop or a religious unlawfully incarcerated and suffering in solitary confinement for twenty or more years with only the rosary to pray on his fingers may in fact be doing a greater work than a bishop who is living in the consolations of obvious success and great recognition for governing and running his diocese. But in living through a grave situation of duress, the suffering person is probably living with special infusions of the gifts of the Holy Spirit, which sustains his ability to live in isolation and loneliness, without honors or tangible accomplishments, perhaps even with rejections and false accusations about his work. He may be doing more for a diocese or dioceses than a bishop living in the lap of success because of his charisms of administration and teaching.

The Final Problem of Pride

Both priests and bishops need reminding that it takes more charity to do difficult works properly than lesser works, and that for most persons, simple and hidden works can quite often be accomplished with more intense charity than difficult or higher

---

[5] In religious life, desire for higher rank means wanting to be a mother general for a religious woman or an abbot or a provincial for male religious.

external works done for mixed motives. One does not need to have money, fame or honor in order to grow in charity. As one grows deeper in the love of God, the more the cross is desired and embraced, without inordinate love for higher office or promotion. And quite often, doing humble tasks with great charity is more praiseworthy from the point of view of God, than doing a greater work with much self-inflation penetrating the work. St. Augustine reminds us in his Rule, that "pride can enter even a good work." Nevertheless, God calls some to great holiness which also entails great works and much fame but it does not go to their heads in pride, vainglory or arrogance.

Finally, what is pride? Pride is the inordinate desire to excel:

> Pride means a craving for superiority which is immoderate because not in accord with right reason. Now it is to be observed that superiority results from the possession of a good. This can be looked at in itself, as to where it comes from, and how it is possessed. First, the good in itself; here obviously the greater it is, the more superior the man who has it. But if a man claims for himself more worth than he has, his appetite will be set on what is beyond his measure. Such is the third kind of pride, namely boasting of qualities one does not have (ST II-II 162, 4).

Simply taken, to wish to excel is reasonable when matched according to one's abilities. In some ways, the reasonable love for excellence is the beginning of virtue. But, when disordered, legitimate pride gives birth to vainglory, covetousness (also sometimes named "avarice" by Thomas), and presumption. If pride rules over the soul, it leads to these other vices related to the inordinate desire for the office of bishop. Of vainglory, Thomas says it is "a dangerous sin, not only on account of its gravity, but also because it is a disposition to grave sins, insofar as it renders man presumptuous and too self-confident: and so it gradually disposes a man to lose his inward goods" (ST II-II 132, 5 ad 3).

And from vainglory comes presumption:

> Presumption… comes from vainglory for the very fact of seeking a great deal of personal glory and leads a person to attempt things beyond his powers especially unusual things that tend to stir up greater admiration. Hence Gregory says that presumption of novelties is a daughter to vainglory (ST II-II 21, 4).

But it is clear that "it is a requisite for man's perfection that he should know himself, but not that he should be known by others wherefore it is not to be desired in itself" (II-II 132, 1 ad 3). Thomas will go on to qualify his assertions by affirming that honor can be desired for the sake of God's glory, or for the sake of others to help them become better persons, or even to aid oneself if it leads to one's perseverance in good works.

Again, if one is in the grip of pride, presumption and vainglory, then the yearning for the office of bishop can be prompted by one's inordinate desire to excel in good works, thinking one's own powers can do the job, or to achieve recognition which leads to dominating others. This seeking can be the result of covetousness also because it can be "an immoderate desire for high places where prominence is immoderately sought after" (II-II 118, 1).

Seeking Higher Offices in Religious Life?

Does Thomas' analysis stand up to the question of seeking "promotions" in religious life, that is, can one desire to have a higher position within a religious institute? The answer from Thomas' point of view is yes, provided the desire is not motivated by pride, presumption, vainglory or even avarice. But can one campaign for the job or actively seek it? Campaigning to be an abbot or provincial or even a local superior suggests potential moral problems because of the spiritual nature of the difficult works associated with these offices which are akin to a bishop's office due to the law of the Church concerning "jurisdiction" (or by delegation as happens with women's institutes). Since it is not necessary for salvation to be a major or minor superior, actively pursuing these offices would be the occasion of various sins. Even though one could desire to do the good works of the office, seeking to possess the office would suggest the sin of ambition.

Conclusion

If St. Thomas is correct in his complex analysis of the problem of seeking higher offices within the Church, then his teaching should become part of the ordinary teaching of the Church so that young priests and bishops more clearly know what to do when they become filled with a desire for greater works and higher offices. From one point of view, Thomas will teach that a pusillanimous spirit is worse than a proud spirit when he writes:

> According to its proper species pusillanimity is a graver sin than presumption, since thereby a man withdraws from good things, which is a very great evil according to *Ethics* 4. Presumption, however, is stated to be wicked on account of pride whence it proceeds (ST II-II 133, 2 ad 4).

But many bad choices would be avoided if more priests would refuse offices, assuming they are not commanded, based upon the reality that most candidates do not really understand their capacities, or lack of them, for doing certain works. Many over-estimate themselves, while others under-estimate. Hence, it would be far better if each person sought to remain in his particular place or status until legitimate authority may recognize his special talent for leadership. Meanwhile, becoming worthy of doing the greater works attached to higher offices by being faithful to the duties of one's position in the priestly or religious state is the best course. It is possible that many may do more for the Church by aspirations for higher office, prayer and penance (as the Little Flower did apropos of her keen desire to go to the missions) than actualizing their desire by political campaigns. Leadership, as such, is not necessary for growth in holiness, but a great desire for God is.

Chapter Nine

Priestly Envy: Another Sort of Green

Before turning to St. Thomas Aquinas for help in understanding the teleology or the ends of envy, a few preliminary thoughts are in order. It is important to keep in mind that studying a vice helps everyone clarify the virtues that the particular vice undermines. Justice and fairness is learned at an early age in large families, for example, from the experiences of minor injustice from siblings. Envy is learned quickly from experience as well. It easily undermines the love of neighbor (and eventually God, when known and willed) when someone is honored, and one perceives and feels either from illusion or objective observation that he is somehow slighted. This reaction can happen even if young people do not know it is sinful to wallow in these thoughts. It takes effort for young and old to learn how to rejoice at another's good fortune, such as earning more money, receiving worldly honors or possessing supernatural gifts. Meditation and contemplation are the twin sources for learning how to rise above feelings of envy and to affirm the gifts, virtues, and honors of others which one may not have. A true virtue which facilitates and activates holy actions can come about only with doing actions aimed at what is right in their object, circumstances and motive. One principal guiding light for growing in faith is that God's refusal to give a favor, good fortune or desired blessing is often a gift in disguise because only he knows what is best for anyone in light of his plans for each person.

While it is true that understanding virtue motivates people

more than understanding vice, it is also important that priests have a knowledge of the capital vices in order to prevent these viruses from infecting the soul and unwittingly make virtue either non-existent or causing individuals to live their lives in the illusion of "not having a clue" about what is going on in their souls. Pride and vainglory are perhaps the most hidden of the capital vices while envy is more "up front" and easily recognizable.

The Role of Sorrow or Distress

Everyone is so designed by creation that sorrow and sadness are simply a part of life. Despair as an emotion is also a part of life too, but it deals with hopeless situations and causes one to cease striving for a particular goal. This may be morally good, or morally evil when against the theological virtue of hope. The emotion of despair in not achieving a goal set for oneself can also exist with the emotion of sadness.

When we look at the emotional makeup of humanity, we see that we are fashioned for love as the primary emotion. Human nature is filled with inclinations to many fundamental goods which, when pursued according to reason and faith, can perfect us. Some of these loves are eventually seen through reflection upon faith and experience to be morally upright or truly perfective, while others are discerned to be disordered, a disorientation that undermines our persons, though sometimes unknowingly. When we achieve the quest of a particular good we desire, such as a degree at a university, then we are somewhat jubilant and at rest. However, when we find ourselves in the middle of evils (physical, psychological or moral) such as guilt, which we cannot get rid of at will, we normally experience sorrow.

Sometimes, large doses of sorrow at an early age can lead to a pessimistic and overly critical outlook on life, a spirit of bitterness about people and the Church both in particular and in general. We can develop the attitudes of looking for the dark side of people and institutions. Parents who are always critical of the way their children do things (or worse, do not make them feel good about their very being) also encourage this problem. They may unwittingly generate negative feelings within their children's very selves.

What Is the Passion or Emotion of Sadness?

Some fans become saddened when their favorite football team loses. Rich and poor alike become disappointed, among other things, when the food in a restaurant or home tastes terrible. Other forms of sadness occur when a child or a spouse dies or becomes seriously ill, or a friend chooses to be a personal enemy for one reason or another. Similarly, experiencing rejection by a friend, feeling alienated in a different culture, lack of success in a particular endeavor, mistakes in judgment leading to feelings of inadequacy, being made fun of, or losing an argument, can also produce the emotion of sadness and perhaps anger as well. Anytime human beings lose something significant in their lives, they become sad over losing that particular good. Since the emotions are linked to the body, even clinical depression can be listed as a species of sadness. Loneliness too can lead to brooding over the past which in turn can breed sadness. These feelings have the potential of being turned into the stuff of holiness or the pathways to vice. If, however, with the help of grace, reason and faith can enter into these negative experiences and stamp the feelings with a higher meaning, then several virtues expand.

This emotion of sadness can be morally good or morally evil depending upon the motive and the moral object of a particular action. If I were to try to rob a bank, and failed, the sadness would be sinful since the moral objective of the act was sinful. If another were trying to preach a fine homily but unwittingly made blunders, his sadness at the outcome would be real even though his attempt was morally upright. Guilt over evil deeds is also a species of sadness. But what about envy or sadness over another's good fortune? Is this discontent always a sin or can it ever be reasonable as well? Our Master, St. Thomas Aquinas has some profound insights to offer on these important questions.

St. Thomas following St. John Damascene considers envy a kind of species of sorrow over another's good. On the face of things this seems odd, for why should another's good be an occasion of sadness? Thomas answers in the following way:

> Now this happens in two ways. A man may be sad about another's good, first, when that good threatens him with real danger of hurt. For example, a man grieves over his enemy's prosperity for fear lest he may do him some harm. Sadness of this type is not envy. It is more an effect of fear, as Aristotle observes.

> In the other way a man may regard another's good as his own evil when it diminishes his renown or excellence. Then envy is discontent over another's good. Consequently men are especially envious of *those goods where glory lies, goods which bring honor and esteem*, as Aristotle says (ST II-II 36, 1).

It happens at some point to all men in Holy Orders that they will experience the first movements of envy when another receives an honor for his priestly life, such as an important governmental position in the diocese or an honorary title such as "monsignor" or some other special award by the bishop. Or perhaps, in an election for a position on the priests' council, others who did not receive a single vote may feel an movement of animus toward others who did. They may feel slighted and discontented because they believe they more than others deserved those "goods" of recognition (as they perceive them to be) and a seat on the council. While these priests may be quite correct in their appraisal about their being more deserving, why are these feeling being stirred up in their souls? Perhaps they feel they are not being appreciated by their bishop, superiors or fellow priests. Yet what causes this problem? And what about others who simply do not care about any of these honors? The main difficulty with those who feel hurt may be due in many cases, but not all, to appearances generating false desires. Thomas gives us some insight on these issues: "Since envy is about another's renown in so far as it seemingly diminishes the renown a man wants, it follows that he is envious only of those whom he wants to rival or surpass in reputation" (Ibid., ad 2).

Vainglory and Envy

If Thomas is correct about the motivation for envy, then it is a by-product in a person who seeks glory in a disordered manner. Such disorder is termed "vainglory" in the Thomistic tradition. Thomas pertinently remarks as an aside that a "man does not envy the people who are out of reach in place, or time or style of life" (Ibid.). He gives the example of a commoner who would be "crazy" to envy a king or a king, a commoner. Rather, one envies "the people near him, he wants equality with them or even to outdo them, since it goes against the grain to have them of better repute than he is. That is the ground of the discontent. On the other hand, similar qualities in another cause delight when they are consonant with one's will" (Ibid.). As we shall see later, this last point holds a great solution to the problem of envy for it concurs with divine love.

In the previous article on envy, the Common Doctor goes on to show that only those who are vain become envious. This is distinct from simple first movements or stirrings:

> No one strives for mastery in matters where he is very deficient. He does not envy those who surpass him there. But if it is by little [matters], then it seems that he may equal them, and so he makes an effort. If in

this he is disappointed because the other is rated higher, then he grieves. **That is why those ambitious of glory are more envious**. Likewise the pusillanimous are also envious; they look on all things as great, so that whatever good befalls another, they reckon they have been bested in something important. So Scripture says, *Envy kills the little ones*; And Gregory observes that *envy is only possible towards those whom we judge to be better than us in some respect* (ST II-II 36, 1 ad 3).

The Problem of the Petty Mind as a Source of Envy

What does the vice of pusillanimity do to a person and how does it shape his outlook toward others? Pusillanimity is the cowardly or faint-hearted attitude toward any goal, virtue, or project and Thomas provides important insight to this vice, which in turn illuminates the psychology of envy:

Everything opposed to natural inclination is a sin, because it goes against the law of nature. There is, however, in everything a natural tendency to undertake action commensurate with its capability. This is evident in all natural things, whether animate or otherwise. But just as presumption leads someone to exceed his capability by straining after what is greater than he can reach, so pusillanimity causes a man to fall short of his capability when he refuses to extend himself to achieve an aim commensurate with his powers (ST II-II 133, 1).

Thomas then gives the example of the man who buried his one talent (Mt 25:14; Lk 19:12). A person like this inflicts harm on his neighbors only indirectly when he fails to take action which could help his neighbor (Ibid., ad 1). This person in other ways simply refuses to employ his talents and energies to attain virtue (ad 2). Further, due to certain "pettiness of mind", this type of person withdraws from "great aims" (ad 2). Thomas gives no examples here, but he would certainly affirm that people who reject the readily available means for growing in holiness, such as daily prayer and frequenting the sacraments, suffer from a "pettiness of mind." The fear of failure coupled with a false appraisal of his talents and gifts results in the small-minded person falsely "holding back from the greatness of which he is worthy" (ad 2). This wrong appraisal is also a lack of true humility which looks to what one is really capable of accomplishing. Mental laziness may also be the source of one's failure honestly to examine one's capacities in order to "achieve what lies within one's powers" (ad 1). This is a kind of withdrawal "from what is good" (ad 4) and leads to a lifetime of stagnation in the growth of virtue.

The pusillanimous priest can be the one who thinks he is not capable of writing a thesis, much less organizing a parish, and so neither expends himself at study nor in the confessional, nor answering his phone messages or mail, nor at working hard to prepare his homilies. Seeking his own comforts, he will escape into what is easy, namely, games or television:

> In amusement there are two things to be considered; first, pleasure — and in this context to be inordinately devoted to amusement is against the true idea of play; second, a certain relaxation or rest, which is opposed to hard work. So just as inability to endure exacting work is characteristic of softness, so also is excessive desire for amusing games or for any other kind of relaxation (ST II-II 138, 1 ad 3).

Now the point that Aquinas was making earlier is that the pusillanimous person is also quite likely to become envious because he does not reach the goals that others around him are achieving. In his *Commentary on Job*, Thomas has a pithy sentence which sums up his idea of the relationship between envy and pusillanimity: "It is, however, the mark of smallness of spirit that someone should think that he cannot prosper among others who are prospering."[1] That smallness of mind leads one to believe that others around him should be as he is. The cause of this "smallness of mind" is the willful failure to see the signs of one's gifts and the call to holiness which actualizes these gifts for the glory of God. Thomas also makes some keen observations regarding the similarity and dissimilarity in persons that relate to this problem in his treatment of the emotion of love.

In discussing the cause of love, Thomas makes the point that "potters quarrel with each other — because one is a threat to the other's business; and 'proud men quarrel' because one may deprive the other of the status they both covet" (ST II-II 27, 3). Even though persons with "small minds" and pusillanimous spirits have the potency for great aims and goals due to their natural or supernatural talents, they choose to be envious because they want others to share in their defective attitudes. The reason for the inner conflict is the contradiction between seeds of virtue present in them and their willed neglect of nurturing them. Because they willingly refuse to recognize or actualize their gifts, envy results when they witness others who are given to virtuous acts which they recognize however dimly could be in them. If they would put more effort into prayer and action, they too could also achieve ends, goals and goods which are deserving honor.

Opportunities Never Given

Another cause of envy occurs when certain goods are lost. Thomas observes:

---

[1] Thomas Aquinas, *The Literal Exposition On Job: A Scriptural Commentary Concerning Divine Providence*, Anthony Damico, tr. and Martin D. Yaffe, ed. (Atlanta, Georgia: Scholars Press, 1989), p. 128.

The memory of goods we have had in the past causes pleasure if we dwell on the fact that we once had them; it causes pain if we dwell on the fact that we have lost them; it causes envy when we consider that someone else has them, since that more than anything else seems to lessen our reputation. So Aristotle said that the *old envy the young; those who have spent much in order to get something envy those who have got it by spending only a little.* They are sad about losing their goods and about others getting goods (ST II-II 27, 3 ad 4).

What happens here is quite clearly illustrated in priestly life as well. A new parochial vicar arrives who may have a great talent for preaching and teaching, or he may have a licentiate or doctorate. If the pastor may have none of these gifts or titles he may begin to develop an envious disposition. Additionally, many other elements can interfere with interpersonal relationships, for as one ages, health, energy, creativity issues may emerge, and thus envy can set in because the pastor did not have the opportunities which the young priest was given. He can begin to feel sorry for himself, especially if the younger man is popular and praised a great deal by the parishioners.

When Is Discontent at Another's Good Fortune Not a Sin?

From another point of view, not all discontent with another's success or fame, and the acceptance or rejoicing over someone's downfall, is necessarily sinful:

> On this Gregory remarks that *it happens frequently that without loss of charity we may rejoice over the downfall of an enemy, or even be sad over his glory without committing the sin of envy. At his fall we believe others will take over with greater right; at his success we dread that many may have to suffer unjustly* (ST II-II 27, 2).

Likewise, in the same article, we learn that sadness over someone's good fortune may also not be sinful for other reasons:

> Secondly, we may be discontented about another's good, not because he has it but rather because we do not. Speaking strictly, this is zealous imitation. If it is about virtuous goods it is laudable. Scripture says, *Be jealous for spiritual gifts.* If it is about temporal goods it may or may not be sinful (Ibid.).

In other words, the humility, patience or wisdom of another may inspire one to aim for these virtues as well.

Thomas next shows why this discontent may or may not be a sin. His understanding of sadness and solution to problems over another's good fortune, however, requires a great deal of faith to handle one's emotions:

> Thirdly, a man may be discontented about another's good when he is unworthy of it. This discontent cannot rise from truly virtuous blessings since these make a man righteous; rather it is about riches, as Aristotle says, and about those things which can come both to the worthy and unworthy alike. He calls this sadness *nemesis* and says it belongs to good morals. He says this because he was considering temporal goods in themselves, inasmuch as they seem wonderful to people who look not to eternity. But the teaching of faith tells us that when good things come to sinners they are, according to God's just dispositions, for their correction or condemnation, and are nothing in comparison to what is in store for the just. For this reason discontent is prohibited in sacred Scripture: *Be not envious of evil doers nor envy them that work iniquity* (Ps 37:1), and again, *My feet were on the point of stumbling; envy the arrogant as I did, and watching the wicked get rich* (Ps 73:2) (Ibid.).

It does happen from time to time in ecclesial life that less capable men are nominated to be bishops or pastors and others know this and become reasonably sad because they fear the damage that will ensue to a diocese or a parish. It takes a great deal of faith to surrender to divine providence and accept the reality which God alone has control over. If Yahweh himself could choose a person as king (Saul: 1 S 9:17-19) who would become a disaster morally speaking, no one need be surprised if bishops or priests who do not have all the prerequisites for sound leadership are chosen by higher authority. The permissive will of God is inscrutable since we know hardly at all the reasons for such permissions — such as Jesus choosing a Judas.

The Precise Sin of Envy Itself

In the fourth paragraph of the same article, Thomas concludes his discussion by stating what properly belongs to envy as a sin:

> Fourthly, we can be discontented about another's good insofar as that surpasses ours. This properly is envy; and it is always wrong. As also Aristotle states, because it is to grieve over what should make us rejoice, namely, our neighbor's good (ST II-II 27, 4).

In conclusion to these distinctions, it is seen that there can be a reasonable feeling of holy discontent which motivates a zeal to advance in virtue within oneself and with one's friends and neighbors. Additionally a sadness for our neighbor's good fortune can reasonably emerge if we perceive that his possession of a particular good will be to the real detriment of ourselves or others; such a feeling may not be sinful. Finally, a sinful discontent may occur over someone's good when it is seen as an evil to us simply because it surpasses us in some way. This is strictly speaking where the sin of envy develops. Thomas further nuances this when he says that "grief over another's prosperity is envy itself when it arises precisely because the success enhances the other's good name and this lessens the envious person's own sense of self-worth and good name" (ST II-II 36, 4 ad 3).

Further on in article three, Aquinas citing Aristotle makes the point that envious people are not "men of mercy, nor are merciful characters men of envy" (II-II 36, 3 ad 3). Envy is an enemy of charity because it becomes disconsolate over "the good of those who deserve it." Their good should lead to rejoicing and affirmation of others as part of charity's responsibilities. Envy will also set someone up against a merciful spirit when the envied person experiences harm in some way and the envious person will not come to help him. Worse still, envy can be a sin against the Holy Spirit when someone "sorrows not only over the good of one's neighbor, but the very increase of God's grace… since by it in a certain way a man envies the Holy Spirit, who is glorified in his works" (II-II 36, 4 ad 2).

The By-Products of Envy

In article four, Thomas explains why envy is a capital sin, that is, a kind of a sin which helps other sins come in its wake, by using the assertions of Gregory the Great:

> From envy comes hatred, gossip, detraction, gloating over our neighbors' hard luck, and being sore at his success (II-II 36, 4, obj. 3).

Detraction which is sometimes called "backbiting" or "calumny" attempts to injure another's character by belittling someone in secret causing others to have a "bad opinion of the person about whom he is spreading his secret tales" so as to take away another's reputation (II-II 73, 1). One can do this either by lying about a person's character, exaggerating his weaknesses, telling his secrets, accusing him of bad intentions in his good deeds, denying his good qualities when he is being verbally attacked, or being silent in a malicious way about his good qualities (II-II 73, 1 ad 3). This act of detraction is considered to be a grave sin in its species because it wilfully injures a person's reputation and thus prevents him from doing many good deeds (II-II 73, 2). It is not a sin however, when the truth needs to be told in a confidential manner to a higher authority for the sake of the individual himself or the common good of the Church. However, even this makes the envious person feel good.

Gossip, which translates *susurratio* or "whispering" goes beyond harming a person's reputation to the desire to split up friendships. This is an even a worse sin objectively since "*a friend is better than honor and to be loved is better than to be honored*" according to Aristotle (II-II 74, 1 & 2).

Hatred must be examined first as an emotion before we can turn to what it means to hate one's neighbor as an outcome of envy. In the *Summa Theologiae* II-II 29, 1-6, Thomas writes about the emotion of hatred. His understanding of this emotion (or as he prefers to call it, "a passion") is simply that "hatred is contrary to love." Good is the object of love and hatred is the object of evil. Where there is pleasure, there is the emotion of love behind it because "everything is naturally in harmony with what is agreeable to it, and this constitutes 'natural love': similarly, it is naturally out of harmony with that which is alien or detrimental to it; and this constitutes 'natural hatred.'"[29] The emotion of hatred is not a sin unless it becomes hatred of God or neighbor. This conversion can be a consequence of envy. Thomas will explain how.

Turning to the *Summa Theologiae*, II-II 34, 6, the Master shows clearly how envy overflows into hatred. For we experience sorrow because we perceive an evil which we feel in another human person. And yet, "envy is sorrow, i.e., sorrow over our neighbor's blessings, and sorrow is hateful to us. Thus out of envy comes hatred." The sin of hatred, which emerges from envy toward one's neighbor falsely appraised as evil to us, consists in wishing evil for its own sake against him because his "disposition or character is not to our liking" (*De Malo*, 12, 4). The person filled with wrongful hate wishes evil for its own sake upon another which in turn will lead to unjust acts; immoral hatred is an evil disposition which does not care "howsoever undeservedly evil befalls the person he hates" (ST II-II 34, 6 ad 3). One might also hate God since he inflicts just punishment for sin thus resulting in the hatred of the very justice of God (II-II 34, 2 ad 3). Hating God is found in every sin against the Holy Spirit (II-II 34, 2).

The final consequence of envy is gloating over another's misfortune. This is "not directly the same as envy, but is a result, since despondency over our neighbor's good (which is envy) gives rise to pleasure over his evil" (II-II 36, 4 ad 3). When the envied bishop, superior, or pastor fails in his mission by his own fault, or diminishes his reputation from bad decisions, or even becomes incapacitated, the envious person is filled with glee instead of compassion for the man's downfall. Perhaps this is one of the great tragedies of our present time: the hidden sins of envy by the gloaters over the downfall of bishops and priests. They may have been envied in their rise and now these same people delight in their misfortunes, putting their own souls in jeopardy for their lack of mercy.

Conclusion

The first movements of sinful envy are signs of weakness, and so, are opportunities for facing oneself, a reality check about what we consider to be of importance in the spiritual life. Quite often, these hints show that we have placed our priorities into a false hierarchy and need to accept the providence of God as it really is and not as we wish it to be. Perhaps if we were honored or rewarded here and now we would be hindered in growing in the love of God because of our self-inflation. Perhaps our time has yet to come and we need more purification before certain goods are given to us by divine providence, if we are to receive them at all. We can often daydream too much about such gifts in moments when we would do more good to be studying the Trinity or Marian theology. Dreaming (or as St. Josemaria Escrivá puts it "mystical wishful thinking") too much of these things can actualize, not the proclamation of the kingdom of heaven but rather the kingdom of one's disordered self-love to the detriment of humble and merciful charity toward others. Envy is the stuff which cuts off this charity and stops our progress in the spiritual life, even killing it temporarily until we repent.

The man of divine love should ordinarily affirm and rejoice in the good fortune and graces that his neighbors are given because as he does so, he encourages others to accept their call, role or mission in order to help them do what their talents and gifts demand of them. Applying the scholastic axiom "Action follows being," we can see that congratulating and rejoicing over others' good fortune is meant to stimulate them to accomplish the destiny that God has given them by showering them with his gifts. Anything less than that can harm their mission as well as our own.

Chapter Ten

Avarice: Persons Becoming Like the Material Goods They Crave

Human beings are designed for beatitude or happiness. The *Catechism* witnesses to this fact when it teaches:

> 1718. The Beatitudes respond to the natural desire for happiness. This desire is of divine origin: God has placed it in the human heart in order to draw man to the One who alone can fulfill it:
> We all want to live happily; in the whole human race there is no one who does not assent to this proposition, even before it is fully articulated.

Two of the vices we have already pondered, pride and vainglory, look to some "property of happiness" that all desire (ST I-II 84, 4). These two vices, although involved in attaining happiness, falsely promise the perfection of excellence and renown and are only chimeras of happiness. Since happiness also involves "self-sufficiency," riches promise an inducement to happiness (Ibid.). The vice called avarice elicits an unreasonable desire for money and the material things which money can buy. The Church has spoken quite pointedly about conquering this vice by giving some general principles for personal motivation as we see in the *Catechism of the Catholic Church* (emphases throughout the chapter are mine):

2403. The *right to private property*, acquired or received in a just way, does not do away with the original gift of the earth to the whole of mankind. **The universal destination of goods remains primordial**, even if the promotion of the common good requires respect for the right to private property and its exercise.

2404. In his use of things man should regard the external goods he legitimately owns not merely as exclusive to himself but common to others also, in the sense that they can benefit others as well as himself [187 GS 69 #1].

The ownership of any property makes its holder a steward of Providence, with the task of making it fruitful and communicating its benefits to others, first of all his family.

St. Thomas Aquinas himself when discussing the question of doing penance for sins after confession teaches that the chief work of satisfaction for sin is almsgiving which directly counters avarice and becomes a work of mercy, a virtue linked immediately to charity (ST *Suppl.* 14, 4; 15, 3 ad 3).

Foundations for Sinning

It seems odd that pride and vainglory can so wound a person's virtue by the power of these desires, that St. Paul called covetousness the root of all evils (1 Tm 6:10), and yet St. Thomas teaches that pride is the beginning of all sin (ST I-II 84, 4). How can we explain these seemingly opposing views?

Every sin involves a turning toward a changeable good in a disordered way. This in turn disposes a person for a slow or total turning from God through venial and mortal sin. It makes sense to say that "because of riches a person acquires the power to commit any kind of sin, of satisfying his desires for every sort of sin; for money helps a man to obtain all manner of temporal goods" (Ibid.). Therefore, avarice is *a kind of root* for sin as a turning unreasonably to material goods.

On the other hand, the sin of pride is called the *beginning of all sin* because it is concerned with a "turning away from God, whose command man refuses to obey. Because the nature of moral evil begins in turning away from God, pride is called sin's 'beginning'" (I-II 84, 2). Each vice, therefore, in its own way, is a kind of mutual foundation for understanding the causes and meaning of sin in general.

Material Goods and the Spirit of Poverty

Material things are goods necessary for living the good life of virtue. If people are sick, hungry or cold, virtue becomes very difficult, though not impossible by special graces from God, given man's fallen nature. Like the emotions, the possession and use of material things can get out of hand. Instead of utilizing them for the glory of God, the human person can become the slave to things, thinking that the more he has the better a person he will become. In many ways, the social teaching of the Church is about curing this problem of wanting to possess things for their own sakes. Even the vow of poverty professed by religious is a frontal assault on avarice. The diocesan priest does not make a vow of poverty, but he like all the Christian faithful is called to live the spirit of poverty. As the *Catechism* so well expresses it:

> 2544. Jesus enjoins his disciples to prefer him to everything and everyone, and bids them "renounce all that [they have]" for his sake and that of the Gospel. Shortly before his passion he gave them the example of the poor widow of Jerusalem who, out of her poverty, gave all that she had to live on. The precept of

detachment from riches is obligatory for entrance into the Kingdom of heaven.

2545. All Christ's faithful are to "direct their affections rightly, lest they be hindered in their pursuit of perfect charity by the use of worldly things and by an adherence to riches which is contrary to the spirit of evangelical poverty."

This detachment is the result of the struggle to control ones' excessive inner desires for material things and also an attempt to share one's possessions with others as circumstances dictate.

2548. Desire for true happiness frees man from his immoderate attachment to the goods of this world so that he can find his fulfillment in the vision and beatitude of God. "The promise [of seeing God] surpasses all beatitude.... In Scripture, to see is to possess.... Whoever sees God has obtained all the goods of which he can conceive" [343].

2549. It remains for the holy people to struggle, with grace from on high, to obtain the good things God promises. In order to possess and contemplate God, Christ's faithful mortify their cravings and, with the grace of God, prevail over the seductions of pleasure and power.

The Struggle Against Avarice and Toward Virtue

Material things can be desired reasonably or to such a degree that they become ends in themselves which in turn blinds the spirit to the true needs of self and others. Mortifying the excessive cravings for material things does not mean killing the desire, but moderating it so that the soul does not become enslaved to possessions. As with any enemy of virtuous living, effort is necessary to overcome avarice, the enemy of many virtues toward our neighbor,

St. Thomas situates avarice, the opposite vice of prodigality, under the rubric of justice. Both vices undermine the virtue of liberality. Justice means a prompt will to give people what is their due or their right as persons either by nature, by promise, or civil law. Avarice clogs this ability since it looks to things before people. It is also called by Aquinas the root of all evil or a foundational sin of self-love (ST I-II 84, 1). Throughout *Summa Theologiae* II-II 118, he shows us its ability to set a will against human rights and dignity. While the commonplace objections to the first article deserve a reading in themselves, his reply is very clear:

> …[M]aterial goods have the quality of usefulness towards an end. Consequently the human good in them consists in a determinate measure, namely that a person seek to possess material wealth to the degree that it is necessary to a life suited to his station. The sin is to go beyond this measure, namely the will to acquire or to hoard material goods excessively. The meaning of avarice, defined as *unchecked love to possess*, involves this and so avarice clearly is sinful (ST II-II 118, 1).

Likewise, the *Catechism* warns: "The disordered desire for money cannot but produce perverse effects. It is one of the causes of the many conflicts which disturb the social order" (CCC 2424).

Most vices have one element in common, namely, that desires and other passions are let loose and unchecked by reason and faith. Only feeling rules the soul rather than moral truth directed by principles. Moreover, rationalizations in favor of any sin result in the idea that desires for any good whatsoever are natural. The Common Doctor replies:

The tendencies of nature have to be controlled in accord with reason which has primacy in man's nature. On this account even if old people, with the breakdown of nature, do more greedily seek compensation in material possessions, just as anyone in need attempts to make up for it, still they are not excused from sin when, in regard to riches, they go beyond the measure called for by reason (ST II-II 118, 1).

In practice, there is a certain relativity with these ideas because that which may be necessary and helpful for one may be excessive for another person. Most people, however, tend to go to the excess rather than the defective side in this desire for things over the desire for holiness or intimacy with the Triune God.

Two Directions of Avarice and Their Outcomes

There are also two tendencies that are involved in the sin of avarice: "getting and keeping" (ST II-II 118, 3). Some people have no compunction about stealing people's property. Others may never actually steal anything, but their inner attachment to wealth may be to such a degree that they give little or nothing to others. (This, as will be seen, is the stuff of the virtue of liberality.) For this reason the *Catechism* warns the faithful by stating: "Love of the poor is incompatible with immoderate love of riches or their selfish use" (2445). When this extreme love for material goods takes place, the other timely principle limps in people's hearts: "When we attend to the needs of those in want, we give them what is theirs, not ours. More than performing works of mercy, we are paying a debt of justice" (2446).

Following St. Gregory the Great, St. Thomas calls the other capital sins the daughters of avarice. However, Gregory also uses the metaphor of "the army of avarice" as well to indicate the many other vices that flow from it: treachery, fraud, falsehood, perjury, restlessness, violence and callousness to mercy. Using the analysis that avarice goes too far in getting and keeping, Thomas shows how this vice gives birth to its daughters:

> First of all it (avarice) goes too far in keeping. In this regard callousness to mercy is born of avarice in that a person's heart is not so softened by mercy as to come to the aid of the wretched out of his own resources.

> Secondly, it is the part of avarice to go too far in getting. In this regard avarice can be looked on in two ways, and first as it is in the heart. Thus restlessness issues from avarice in that this engenders anxiety and undue worry in a person; *a covetous man shall not be satisfied with money* (Ecclesiastes 6:9) (ST II-II 118, 8).[1]

While it should be noted here that there is such a quality as reasonable anxiety or worry (a species of fear), in his treatment of prudence Thomas explains why undue or unreasonable anxiety is wrong:

> Providence [is God's care of us and all our needs], of which unbelievers are ignorant, and so are preoccupied with the pursuit of earthly goods. He (Our Lord) concludes, therefore, that our first care should be for spiritual goods, while yet hoping that temporal goods will be forthcoming provided we do what we ought (ST II-II 55, 6).

Contrary to dissenting theologians, this passage indicates that not all of morality taught by revelation can be articulated and held simply by human reason. As is seen in this passage, faith is involved or penetrates the moral life and elevates it to a higher

---

[1] We also saw how a lack of mercy affects the envious person when someone he envies is in trouble and he delights in his ill fortune instead of being merciful. But this can also be an effect of lust, acedia and anger as well.

level than that attainable by human reasoning. This seems to be what the Church has in mind when the *Catechism* states:

> The Lord grieves over the rich, because they find their consolation in the abundance of goods. Let the proud seek and love earthly kingdoms, but "blessed are the poor in spirit for theirs is the Kingdom of heaven." **Abandonment to the providence of the Father in heaven** frees us from anxiety about tomorrow. Trust in God is a preparation for the blessedness of the poor. They shall see God (2547).

So Thomas reprises in this section on prudence what he will teach later in the same *Summa*:

> Temporal goods are subject to man that he may use them according to his needs, not that he should make them his main purpose or be overly anxious about them (ST II-II 55, 6 ad 1).

Further Nuances on Planning for the Future

However, the Common Doctor following Augustine is also realistic about anxiety and worry and teaches that there is an attitude of due solicitude about the future. These texts speak for themselves:

> Duly looking to the future belongs to prudence, yet such forethought and concern would be inordinate were a person to make temporal things, to which terms "past" and "present" apply, his purpose in life, or were he to seek superfluities beyond the needs of his present life or anticipate the fitting time for solicitude (ST II-II 55, 8 ad 2).

> Augustine tells us that when we see a servant of God

taking precautions so as not to fall into want of necessities, we should not judge him to be solicitous for tomorrow. Our Lord himself, as an example to us, deigned to keep a purse, and as we read in *Acts* that the apostles procured the needs of livelihood for the future in view of a threatened famine. Our Lord, then, does not disapprove of one who takes care of these things according to human custom, but of one who does so to fight against God (II-II 55, 8 ad 3).

In other words, reasonable solicitude is neither avarice nor imprudent when the correct motives and attitudes are informing financial or temporal decisions, whereas the prodigal person lacks this prudence and irresponsibly spends money quite often without thought of tomorrow (II-II 119, 1 & 2).

Continuing his analysis of avarice, Aquinas says:

In another way avarice can be viewed as to its effect, whereby in order to acquire wealth the man of greed employs now force — which entails violence; now deceit. Should the deceit be perpetrated verbally, where there is simple assertion, we have falsehood; where there is confirmation by oath, perjury. If the deceit is accomplished by deed, when it centers upon some object, it is fraud; on persons, treachery, as is clear from Judas' betrayal of Christ out of greed (ST II-II 118, 8).

Cautionary Note for Priestly Spirituality

At this point, it is necessary to point out that priests and bishops alike can become avaricious not only for their own personal wealth but also for the wealth of their parishes or dioceses. At a certain point, savings that are no longer necessary for the maintenance and upkeep of the parish should be put out on loan to less fortunate parishes. Sometimes, future pastors can desire to be in charge of rich parishes so that they do not have to work so hard at managing the assets of the church and can relax rather than be reasonably solicitous. Finally, priests can be so worried about their retirement that they obsess about their investments in the stock markets to the detriment of contemplation or the salvation of souls. What begins as a legitimate concern for the future can lead one to become imperceptibly miserly as one advances to old age. What are superfluities in the younger years can become demands in one's later years. So, instead of seeing money as something belonging to Christ and given to the priest on loan, it can become a kind of end in itself through undue attachment. Hence, the need for growing in the virtue of liberality arises which reasonably takes into account one's authentic needs.

The Aim of Conquering Avarice:
Organized Mercy as the Justice of the Kingdom

Liberality, according to St. Thomas is at the heart of the social teaching of the Church. This centrality is affirmed by the many theologians of the Church's social teaching as well as in the official Church documents of the past decades.[2] We find a profound understanding of this virtue in Aquinas as something to be lived and not merely exercised at random:

> As Ambrose and Basil say, a surplus of wealth is granted to some people by God so that they may gain **the merit of good stewardship**. Accordingly, since one person can get along on little, **the liberal man commendably spends more on others than on self**. A

---

[2]   T.C. O'Brien will translate *liberalitas* as generosity but I will stick to the more literal translation because the word generosity implies the notion of favor, whereas liberality in this context is something more than a favor.

person's obligation to take better care of self than of others applies to his spiritual well-being, wherein it is possible for every man to show the main concern for himself. Still, even in regard to temporalities it is no part of being liberal for someone to be so solicitous of others as to have no regard at all for self or family. Hence Ambrose says, *liberality is commendable as long as you do not neglect your own kin, should you know they are in want* (ST II-II 117, 1 ad 1).

Love of self comes second in the hierarchy of loves, love of neighbor comes third, but there is an order to divine love such that family comes next. After these are taken care of, then the merit of "giving" comes to play. The liberal man is bountiful with mercy, lets go of his money and "shows that his spirit is free from attachment to it" (II-II 117, 2). His virtue is an affection for reasonable giving more than just an amount of money that he possesses. Even the poor can possess this virtue. Likewise, the Church's teaching as found in the *Catechism* is quite clear concerning the obligation to give to the poor:

> 2446. St. John Chrysostom vigorously recalls this: "Not to enable the poor to share in our goods is to steal from them and deprive them of life. The goods we possess are not ours, but theirs." "The demands of justice must be satisfied first of all; that which is already due in justice is not to be offered as a gift of charity": **When we attend to the needs of those in want, we give them what is theirs, not ours. More than performing works of mercy, we are paying a debt of justice.**

Virtue usually implies the ability to do something according to faith and reason. In some circles, the virtue of liberality is thought of as the ability to save money. Thomas comes up with a differing viewpoint:

The act distinctive of the liberal man is to use money. The use of money means letting it go. For the acquiring of money is more like a coming to be than a use, and the saving of it more like a habit (that is a disposition or a training for a virtue — the author), since the purpose of the power is to use money. The release of something proceeds from the greater power (*virtus*) the further the distance it is to go, as the example of throwing shows. In this way there is greater virtue behind the releasing of money in giving to others than in spending it on self. Since it is distinctive of virtue, *being itself a form of perfection* (from Aristotle), that it strive especially towards the more perfect, the liberal man is praised especially for giving (ST II-II 117, 4).

It is in the answer to the first objection that we find a further nuance:

Prudence has to protect money against theft or senseless spending. But it takes not less but more prudence to spend wisely than to save wisely, since there are more factors to consider in using a thing, which is compared to movement, than in keeping, which is compared to rest (II-II 117, 4 ad 1).

It is certainly prudent to save but it takes more effort of discerning thought to spend or give, which says a great deal about this virtue. The senseless saving of money can lead to many other vices associated with avarice as too can spending of it (prodigality). Prudent giving does not pertain to justice (II-II 117, 5) nor from civil law, but from an understanding of the meaning of solidarity with one's neighbors which springs up from the law of the gospel. Liberality "is concerned with setting right a person's attitude towards the possession and use of money.... By not being a money lover a person easily uses it for both his own well-being and that of others, as well as for God's honor" (II-II 117,

6). So when the Church teaches about benefitting others in the marketplace, she is appealing, although implicitly, to owners and workers to develop this virtue of liberality as we see again in the *Catechism*:

> 2405. **Goods of production — material or immaterial — such as land, factories, practical or artistic skills, oblige their possessors to employ them in ways that will benefit the greatest number.** Those who hold goods for use and consumption should use them with moderation, reserving the better part for guests, for the sick and the poor.

> 2424. A theory that makes profit the exclusive norm and ultimate end of economic activity is morally unacceptable. The disordered desire for money cannot but produce perverse effects. It is one of the causes of the many conflicts which disturb the social order. A system that "subordinates the basic rights of individuals and of groups to the collective organization of production" is contrary to human dignity. Every practice that reduces persons to nothing more than a means of profit enslaves man, leads to idolizing money, and contributes to the spread of atheism. "You cannot serve God and mammon."

Conclusion

All of this teaching of both Aquinas and the Church has important ramifications for the life and ministry of the priest. If he does not check his inclinations to have more than is necessary or does not see his wealth as a treasure owed to others, then he will not teach these truths to his people. When that happens, then by default he lets the same vice of avarice continue to exist in his people, which also pushes them away from having more children through contraception, and sometimes abortion. It also will harden them against mercy to the poor and even in the workplace. From another standpoint, this vice can undermine one's priestly spirituality because of a fear that collections will go down; he will forego preaching other hard truths of the message of Christ. The great cause for a loss of morale in the recent past has been the sexual abuse scandals and the punitive measures established by the bishops through their particular legislation, strictly or broadly taken. It may very well be the case that the problems of lust with a few of the clergy is much smaller than the problems of avarice. It may also very well be that much of the problem of dissent concerning received norms on sexual ethics was really the problem of a rich Church wanting to grow richer in material things. Only God knows.

Chapter Eleven

Gluttony, a Minor Problem with Potentially Major Consequences

An easier vice to understand than anger or acedia and one less debilitating of the spirit than pride or vainglory is called in Latin *gula* (gluttony), which is a desire for excessive eating and drinking of alcoholic beverages (for the most part in the middle ages, wine and beer). There is no deep analysis of it in the papal magisterium of the Church and the word appears only once in the *Catechism*, in a list of all the other capital vices (CCC 1866). The virtues which keep gluttony in check are most immediately: abstinence, fasting, and sobriety. This vice has different ways of giving into the excessive desire for eating and also drunkenness. Furthermore, gluttony spawns five daughters.

Dieting and Virtue

In the USA, many doctors are worried about the obesity of Americans and the negative consequences of being overweight. In addition, many women and some men seem to suffer from bulimia and anorexia, both psychological conditions involving food. From a Thomistic perspective, overeating is clearer in the abstract than in the concrete. On the other hand, dieting or losing weight is not necessarily a virtue although if the motives are reasonable, lifelong dieting can be a manifestation of the virtue of abstinence whether or not one actually loses weight. Losing weight could however be virtuous if it means conserving one's life. Finally, fasting in the Catholic tradition is to be distinguished from dieting; though *materialiter* they are the same, *formaliter* they are radically different because of the motives involved. It is very important to make these distinctions before discussing the capital vice of gluttony and the virtue it opposes.

The Essence of Gluttony

"Eating is gluttonous when one knowingly exceeds his measure from desire for pleasure" (ST II-II 148, 2 ad 2). This definition from St. Thomas Aquinas helps the moralist or ethicist begin to understand this infection of the spirit which seems to pervade the Western/American culture today. Aquinas teaches that behind this vice is the "desire for pleasure." In another of his works, the *De Malo*, Aquinas presents some interesting objections that help situate the evil involved with this vice of gluttony.

In the first article of question 14 of the *De Malo*, Thomas raises the question: "Whether gluttony is always a sin?" In the first objection Thomas cites Gregory the Great who says: "Because in eating, pleasure is blended with necessity, we fail to discern what necessity itself demands and what pleasure secretly demands." Then he quotes Augustine in the second objection: "Who is there, who does not partake of food a little beyond the limit of his need?" And in the third objection, he references Augustine in his own words: "Where nature and necessity are in control there is no culpability. But nature and necessity move man to an act of gluttony." Finally, in the fourth objection, he argues that "immoderate hunger is an immoderate desire of eating, in which the nature of gluttony consists. But it is not within our power not to be immoderately hungry." The conclusion of all these objections would seem to be that there is no sin in gluttony.

However, in his reply to the objections, St. Thomas begins

by restating that virtue is a rule of reason that must govern external actions and the internal passions or we would say today moods and emotions. He admits the most difficult desire to regulate is that for pleasure, especially natural and necessary pleasures associated with daily life such as food and drink and sex without which human life cannot stay in existence or be passed on to future generations. However, he argues that the sin of gluttony which exceeds (or exceeding) the rule of reason, consists in "an inordinate desire of eating." He further explains referring to Aristotle's *Nicomachean Ethics* in the reply to objection one:

> The rule of reason in these matters is that a person should take food commensurate with the sustenance of nature and the good condition of man and the society of those with whom he lives.... When therefore a person desires and takes food according to this rule, he takes it according to need; but when he exceeds his limit, he transgresses the rule of reason by departing from the mean of virtue to satisfy the desire of pleasure (*De Malo* 14, 1 ad 1).

It is surprising for beginners in moral reasoning to note that not the quantity of food per se is at the heart of this sin but an inordinate "desire." Thomas repeats this idea in the answer to the second objection where he states that even if one is *de facto* wrong about what he or she thinks is necessary for nourishment, "in that case the desire for food is not immoderate because it does not depart from the rule of reason." The quantity of food is however part of the problem because Thomas admits that the departure from what is the mean between excess and defect is knowable. However, when a deviation of desire is slight, it is not easily discernible and will have "little of the nature of sin." Yet he thinks that even this slight sin can be avoided "especially with the help of God" (*De Malo* 14, 1 ad 2). As regards natural necessity then, eating can exceed the rule of reason and so gluttony enters the moral picture of life. Excess of hunger as distinct from the desire for pleasure, however, is not a moral fault, but "rather diminishes or entirely excuses fault" (*De Malo* 14, 1 ad 4).

Nature and Desire Distinguished

In the *Summa Theologiae*, Thomas includes the idea of excessive drinking in the sin of gluttony and further distinguishes the notion of eating too much

> ...so that when a person eats too much, not on account of desire, but from thinking it necessary, he acts from inexperience, not gluttony. Eating is gluttonous when he knowingly exceeds his measure from desire for pleasure (ST II-II 148, 1 ad 2).

The reason why he seems to be so lenient or tolerant in this matter is because there is a double appetite at work in this area, namely, nature's pull for nourishment and the desire for pleasure's pull (II-II 148, 1 ad 3). From these insights, Thomas will be able to answer the next question whether gluttony is a grave sin or not.

When Gluttony Is Gravely Sinful

The Master's analysis of the sin of gluttony is based in part on his earlier treatment in the *Summa* I-II 72, 5 & 88, 1. It is therefore logical for him to say that theoretically one could commit a mortal sin of eating too much if his motive were such that he would be "prepared to break God's commandments in order to find his pleasure" (II-II 148, 2). In other words, making the desire for pleasures of the palate an end in itself makes this sin mortal; anything less is venial. Overeating is usually less culpable because of "our need to take food and because of the difficulty of applying proper discretion and moderation in the matter" (II-II 148, 4). Its gravity will really be seen when it becomes the occasion of other sins (Ibid.). However, eating too much is not the only way that one can be gluttonous. St. Gregory the Great provides five different ways: *sometimes forestalling the hour of need, sometimes seeking sumptuous food, sometimes requiring elaborate dishes, sometimes exceeding in amount of measure of refreshment, and sometimes sins by too hot* (too ardent) *a hunger* (II-II 148, 4 obj. 1).[1] Note however that all these species could be reasonable if not based upon excessive desire.

Gluttony's Daughters

Now, since gluttony is about an outstanding pleasure of the body, it is by default a capital sin spawning five other sins. Because immoderate eating and drinking blunts the sharpness of thinking, the following actions are not reasonable. The first daughter is called uncleanness of body, which in the *Summa* refers to any kind of sexual incontinence. The second is called dullness of sense and a defect of understanding caused by too much food (and drink), which understanding should rule the soul. The third is unseemly joy whereby the emotional state of a person becomes infected because "reason is asleep at the helm" (II-II 148, 4). The fourth is verbosity (idle talk) whereby one's speech is affected because reason fails to weigh its words. The fifth is called "scurrility," which refers to obscene language and gestures whereby someone acts like a buffoon (Ibid.; cf. *De Malo* 14, 4).

Another aspect of gluttony that is sometimes lost in our modern culture is the question of the harm to the body that results from eating too much. Thomas was way ahead of his time when he wrote:

---

[1] This is set forth in a line of verse: Hastily, sumptuously, daintily, too much, greedily from the Latin *prepropere, laute, nimis, ordenter, studiose.*

Nevertheless if someone knowingly were to inflict grave harm on his own body because of his immoderate desire for food by eating too much or by taking harmful foods, he would not be excused from mortal sin (*De Malo* 14, 2 ad 4).

Likewise such reasoning could also be rightly applied to the excessive use of tobacco, alcohol, and other stimulants as contrary to the cardinal virtue of temperance.

Priestly Problems with Gluttony

If one has not learned to curb one's desires for the pleasures of the palate, then living alone or in a wealthy parish can produce a series of problems in this area of life. Since priests do not have families, the meal can take on a certain undue importance in terms of the various species of gluttony that Thomas alluded to in article three. A priest can come to expect nothing but the best cuisine whether in terms of quantity, expense, or the best of condiments to give the food a special relish. It can also set up a problem with one's prayer life as the desire for pleasure can weaken the desire for prayer or contemplation, even if excess in eating and drinking is minor only. It is in looking at the virtues of eating and drinking that one can see more clearly how gluttony can become a subtle enemy to the spiritual life of a priest.

The Virtues Which Check Gluttony

The virtues which bolster the human spirit affecting food and drink (we might add smoking and mild stimulants as well such as coffee or tea) are called by St. Thomas abstinence, fasting, and sobriety. Virtue when properly understood tends to resonate with human nature (although not perfectly due to original sin) since there are natural inclinations to follow what is reasonable.

Abstinence means "either not eating" or "doing without food under regulation of reason" (ST II-II 146, 1). When the latter occurs, then it is a virtue when "joined to knowledge with due respect of the company a man keeps, to his personal dignity and to the requirements of his health" (Ibid.). The craving for food is necessary because we need food to stay alive, but the virtue keeps this craving reasonable. Nevertheless, a certain mean has to be kept as Gregory warns:

> *Frequently when the flesh is restrained more than is just, it is weakened even for the exercise of good works, so that it does not have the strength for prayer and preaching, while it hastens to stifle completely the incentives to vices within itself; and so while we attack the enemy we hate, we also slay the citizen we love (De Malo 14, 1 ad 6).*

Fasting on the other hand is not the same as reasonable eating, but rather it is a form of abstinence which curbs the number of meals in the day (distinguishing what constitutes a full meal and a partial meal) together with the kinds of food that are consumed (usually red meat). The regulations surrounding fasting are a matter of natural law and "a matter for positive laws prescribed by Church authorities, which give a determinate shape to a common duty" (ST II-II 147, 3 ad 1). The particulars of Church law will vary from era to era, country to country. Church law and monastic practice have varied over the centuries in part due to a false understanding as to what constitutes meat (in some centuries web-footed birds were not considered meat) or what is healthy or even what kinds of food may cause lust. Perhaps in our own time, forgoing desserts, salt, sugar and other spices for a few months, or eating foods that are plain but nourishing could be a form of fasting. The present *Code of Canon Law* (§1249- §1253) gives general guidelines about doing penance every Friday and certain other days and times of the year, but leaves it to episcopal conferences to determine the details. Presently, all Fridays of the year are meant to be penitential days, even though the abstinence from meat is not demanded by divine or ecclesiastical law with the exception of Ash Wednesday and Good Friday (although even this is only ecclesiastical law). More importantly, what are the reasons for fasting as seen by Thomas?

The *Summa Theologiae* has a very uncommon common sense approach to fasting. Aquinas begins his analysis by looking at three motives for fasting. It is "First, to bridle the desires of the flesh," which means undermining both lust and gluttony. Second, it enables the mind to rise "more freely to the heights of contemplation." And finally, it makes atonement or "satisfaction for sin" (ST II-II 147, 1). While fasting has legitimate ends, it must not "go so far to deprive nature of its necessary support... or rendering us incapable of discharging our duties" (II-II 147, 1 ad 2).

During the stricter and more legalistic periods in the Church, Thomas' doctrine would have brought more reasonableness into the ascetical priorities of some had it been more widely known. For he teaches that some special reasons can exist which would make fasting unreasonable in particular circumstances. He offers the following justification for being lenient, even allowing people to follow their own judgments if this is supported by custom, and lawful authority is not easily available to dispense from the obligation of fast and abstinence:

> God's commandments are of natural law, of themselves necessary for salvation. Not so, however, the commandments of the Church, which are there because the Church has instituted them. Consequently obstacles can arise which prevent their being kept, and this can be the case with fasting regulations (II-II 147, 4 ad 1).

Put in the modern language of moralists, fasting is a positive obligation which does not always oblige here and now, or it is not intrinsically evil to set aside a fasting law in light of special circumstances. Likewise, Thomas appeals to the common sense of the friars and monks of his time, when he says, contrary to some monastic practices of the not too distant past when scales were present at table to measure out quantities of food,

> The same amount of food cannot be fixed for all on account of differences of bodily constitution; some need more, others less. Nevertheless a single meal is ample for the majority (II-II 147, 6 ad 1).

Today, of course, it is customary to eat three meals a day, even if one is fasting, because of a number of factors bearing on custom, human psychology and the workplace.

Drunkenness as Another Vice of Gluttony

It is not until we see some of the effects of drunkenness that we get a fuller picture of the evil of gluttony because Aquinas does not limit *gula* simply to eating. In the *Summa*, Thomas treats of this problem with only four articles (II-II 150, 1-4), which are valuable from the point of view of theory, but not for pastoral application to individuals. To this end Alcoholics Anonymous has done a great service in its approach to solving the problems of alcoholism, and leading the way for sobriety and treatment of other chemical addictions.

In *Summa* II-II 150, 1, Thomas distinguishes culpable drunkenness from inculpable drunkenness; the latter occurring when a drinker is unaware how strong an alcoholic beverage is and if someone's ignorance is not due to negligence. As in food, the sin is found in an "inordinate desire for the use of wine" not wine in itself. In the answer to the fourth objection, we do find some pastoral insights from Augustine for people who may have no addiction, but need a correction because of excessive feasting and drinking:

> *It seems to me that such things are not to be banished with bitterness, harshness, and high-handedness, but rather by instructing than commanding, by advising not threatening. Such is the course to be followed with most sinners; few are they whose sins are to be visited with severity* (ST II-II 150, 1 ad 4).

Drunkenness however can become a mortal sin when someone "knowingly and willingly deprives himself of the control of reason, the power of adopting right and rejecting wrong" (II-II 150, 2). While knowing this should be enough reason for refraining from excessive drink, "the passion for drink does diminish the fault, for sins of weakness are less grievous than deliberate wickedness" (II-II 150, 4 ad 3).

Sobriety and Temperance

The opposite virtue of drunkenness is traditionally called sobriety. The Latin word, *bria*, implies a measure, especially when drinking alcoholic beverages affecting reason: "[T]heir measured use is most profitable, and excessive addiction, which hampers the sway of reason, even more than excessive eating of food, [is] most harmful" (II-II 149, 2). While Thomas does not elaborate, it is evident from experience that "spirits" tend to foster relaxation, gladden the heart, induce conversation and aid in health when taken moderately. Sobriety then is a special virtue which prevents the human person from acting unreasonably in the use of "spirits" (II-II 149, 3). St. Thomas adds that while drinking wine is not unlawful as such, it may become so "incidentally." He gives examples from the condition of the drinker who cannot take wine's inebriating effects without becoming incapacitated, or whose behavior when drinking may give scandal

(II-II 149, 4). Here and in the next article, Thomas warns that people of greater standing in any community need to be especially sober to fulfill their more weighty duties whether they drink in private or in public.

Conclusion

The ascetical life, as we have seen so far, is not an attempt to kill anything bodily or spiritual in the human person, but rather, is a struggle to order by reason and faith one's appetites, both sensible and spiritual. Contrary to common misconception, as one succeeds in this endeavor, it does not make one joyless or distant from people. Such a false view of the ascetical life leads to Jansenism, and to some extent Manicheanism. Holiness does not mean running away from nature, but ordering nature according to its purposes. Virtue is like a beautiful work of art or music whereby the stuff of these arts, whether paint or melody, lines or harmony and rhythm, are transfused with reason and faith. As one lives the life of virtue, so one disposes oneself to live by the seven gifts of the Holy Spirit or the mystical life. We can never manipulate the gifts but we can be ready to say "yes" to their actualization by the Holy Spirit by not putting up a resistance to his instigations. Even in the ascetical life, these gifts are operative to help us in certain very hard difficulties; their force is episodic unless we are mystics. In the mystical state, these gifts become predominant in one's life, leading us to doing heroic virtuous acts. These smaller virtues we have considered in this chapter, which regulate food and drink, aid in the whole process of growth in the life of Christ. They keep gluttony from clogging the road to holiness, by tempering the appetite and leading the desire for food rather than being led by the desire for pleasure.

Chapter Twelve

Lust and Priestly Celibacy

Some priests and deacons make a vow or a sacred promise of chastity directly to God before they are ordained as transitional deacons; they are usually called members of the consecrated life. Others make a promise of celibacy to their bishop on the day of their ordination to the transitional diaconate; they eventually become diocesan priests or members of Societies of Apostolic Life. Both the vow and the promise can be taken for all the wrong reasons, such as hoping that the Church will change her discipline, thereby rendering both the promise or vow merely conditional, and thereby invalidating at least their state if not Orders itself. Likewise, making these sacred promises from a fear of sex or intense dislike of intimacy with the opposite sex can also harm one's ability to work effectively in the sacred ministry. To appreciate these sacred bonds, one must first look at chastity in the married state. Then one is clearer in understanding the life of perfect chastity, which the priest in the Latin rite is called to, that is, the renunciation of marriage and the avoidance of all sins relating to chastity or continence.

Chaste Marital Acts

To appreciate the importance of the virtue of "perfect" chastity which completely renounces all legitimate sexual activity, it is necessary to understand what conjugal chastity is. To do this we need to rediscover St. Thomas' theology of the authentic marital act as found in the *Supplementum*, composed by his secretary, Bl. Reginald of Piperno, and taken from other writings of Aquinas.[1] In question 41, the best objection to the question of the goodness of the marriage act is found in number 6:

> Further, excess in the passions corrupts virtue. Now there is always excess of pleasure in the marriage act, so much so that it absorbs the reason which is man's principal good, wherefore the Philosopher says (*Ethic.* VII, 11) that "in that act it is impossible to understand anything." Therefore the marriage act is always a sin (*Suppl.* 41, 6).

In the body of his article, he sets up his response to the objection:

> If we suppose the corporeal nature to be created by the good God, we cannot hold that those things which pertain to the preservation of the corporeal nature and to which natures inclines, are universally evil. Therefore, since the inclination to beget offspring whereby the specific nature is preserved by human nature itself, it is impossible to maintain that the act of begetting children is universally unlawful, so that it be impossible to find the mean of virtue therein; unless we suppose, as some are bold enough to assert, that corruptible things were created by an evil god.... [T]his is a most wicked heresy (*Suppl.* 41, 1).

Here he is defending the created order of human nature and is setting up the arguments in favor of marriage itself. The answer to the objection raised herein is now given:

---

[1] The *Supplementum* was translated by the Fathers of the English Dominican Province (New York: Benziger Brothers, 1947). The following texts are based upon their tranlation and my own.

> The excess of passion that corrupts virtue not only
> hinders the act of reason but also destroys the order
> of reason. The intensity of pleasure in the marriage
> act does not do this, since, although at the moment
> of the sexual act a man is not fully in control of him-
> self, he was previously directed by reason to engage
> in the act (*Suppl.* 41, 1 ad 6).

The authentic conjugal act is ordered by choosing its ends, which
can be integrated together: the glory of God (divine charity), the
desire for children to be raised up for heaven (the virtue of religion) or, to render the debt of marriage to one's partner request-
ing the act (the virtue of justice based upon the marital promises).

Some think that what is meritorious by virtue consists in
doing what is difficult. Therefore, since the marriage act affords
great pleasure, it cannot be a meritorious act (*Suppl.* 41, 1 obj.
4). Thomas answers this bad theology by applying his theology
of grace: when any morally good act is done in the state of grace,
even with pleasure, it merits an essential reward since charity
motivates the human action, as distinct from mere acts of man
like a heart-beat or a sneeze. All the goods of marriage render
the marital act blameless even though the pleasure is intense.
This excess is not beyond the bounds of reason nor becomes
immoderate. It is not even a venial sin to take pleasure in this
act nor is it an act of perfection to detest the pleasure because
"pleasure in a good action is good, and in an evil action, evil"
(*Suppl.* 49, 6). However, lustful thoughts or thinking of another
person can corrupt even a good marital act because it undermines
the immediate intention of the act itself. In other words, a lustful act is radically different from an authentic conjugal act.

Chastity Before Marriage

The primary purpose of pre-marital chastity is to develop good and holy marriages. As a teenager masters this powerful impulse before marriage, he is able to master it within marriage and live up to his promises of fidelity, indissolubility, and openness to life and love. This attitude counteracts the temptations of adultery, contraception and abortion, among other sins of the flesh. But, in addition to this great good, pre-marital chastity also brings about a love of the religious and/or priestly life whereby one wants to serve God by transcending the marital state. As Thomas Aquinas argues:

> ...but in the time of grace there is an obligation to insist rather on spiritual propagation for which those living a celibate life are more fitted; and therefore in this state it is considered more virtuous to abstain from the procreative act (*De Malo* 15, 2 ad 3).

Several Consequences of the Promise of Celibacy for Priests

Paul VI's document, *Priestly Celibacy*[2] teaches us about this way of life:

> 27. The priest dedicates himself to the service of the Lord Jesus and of His Mystical Body with complete liberty, which is made easier by his total offering, and he realizes more fully the unity and harmony of the priestly life. (11) His ability increases for listening to the Word of God and for prayer. Indeed, the Word of God, as preserved by the Church, stirs up in the priest, who daily meditates on it, lives it and preaches it to the faithful, echoes that are vibrant and profound.

---

[2] Pope Paul VI, *Priestly Celibacy* (Vatican City: Vatican Press, 1967).

28. Like Christ Himself, His minister is wholly and solely intent on the things of God and the Church (cf. Lk 2:49; 1 Cor 7:32-33), and he imitates the great high Priest who stands in the presence of God ever living to intercede in our favor (Heb 9:24; 7:25). So, he receives joy and encouragement unceasingly from the attentive and devout recitation of the Divine Office, by which he dedicates his voice to the Church who prays together with her Spouse,(12) and he recognizes the necessity of continuing his diligence at prayer, which is the profoundly priestly occupation (Ac 6:4).

Now we are ready to pursue the real meaning of lust which is what the vow of chastity or the promise of celibacy attacks or tries to undermine, not marriage or the marital act itself.

Lust as the Source of False Happiness

Like avarice and gluttony, lust is an inordinate desire, here for sexual pleasure as an end in itself. It is distinct from a desire for an authentic conjugal act. What makes the desire inordinate is the intention of the desire or the external act contrary to the goals and meaning of marriage itself. Thus the desire for marriage and the marital act cannot be lust per se. Referencing St. Augustine, Thomas says "that lust is not the fruit of beautiful and pleasing bodies but of the soul that perversely loves sensual pleasures, to the neglect of temperance, which attaches us to realities far more beautiful and pleasing in their spirituality" (*De Malo* 15, 1). Developing this idea further, he says elsewhere that "The goal of lechery is sexual pleasure, the greatest pleasure to the sensory appetite, and therefore highly desirable, both because of the vehemence of the pleasure and because it is so bound up with our nature" (ST II-II 153, 4).

The traditional arguments in favor of lustful action are

clearly outlined in several lucid objections to what the scriptures and the Church teach concerning adultery and fornication:

> To know a woman sexually is a natural act; therefore considered in itself it is not a sin, just as neither is it a sin to look on her since each of them is the act of a natural power. But to look at a woman who is not one's wife is not a sin. Therefore neither is it a sin to know a woman sexually who is not one's wife (*De Malo* 15, 1 ad 2).

> Augustine says that what food is for the health of the body, intercourse is to the health of the race. Not all inordinate use of food is grave sin, therefore not all inordinate intercourse. This seems to be the case with simple fornication, which is of the kinds of lechery enumerated (ST II-II 154, 2 obj. 6).

Both objections are quashed by prolonged reflection on the meaning of marriage and offspring based in part on an appeal to experience. Without the commitment of marriage, children are not properly taken care of, which is the brunt of the issue throughout the works of Aquinas. The idea comes down to the injustice inflicted upon children born from fornication or adultery. Thomas however, realizes not everyone can understand all the reasons when he says:

> The precepts of the Decalogue were given directly to the people of God; hence they are given in that form in which they are clearly apprehensible to the natural reasons of everyone even the ordinary man. And indeed everyone by natural reason can see immediately that adultery is a sin, and therefore among the precepts of the Decalogue adultery is forbidden; however, fornication and other corrupt practices are forbidden by the subsequent precepts of the law that

were given by God to the people through Moses because the deordination of those acts, since it does not clearly contain by implication an injury to one's neighbor, is not evident to all but only to the wise through whom it ought to be conveyed to the knowledge of others (*De Malo* 15, 2 ad 3).

Nevertheless, when someone understands what the virtue of chastity does for a person, the reasoning about it only adds encouragement to practice it:

The love of chastity can be pleasing not only to him who possesses chastity but also to him who is without the virtue of chastity, inasmuch as man by natural reason esteems the good of virtue and loves it and is attracted by it even if he does not have it (*De Malo* 15, 2 ad 5).

The Daughters of Lust

Although Thomas relies on Gregory's enumeration of the daughters of lust, Thomas appeals to experience again to understand how these effects of vice undermine the human spirit. There are eight effects: blindness of mind, thoughtlessness, inconstancy, temerity, self-love, hatred of God, love of the present world, and despair of a future world (*De Malo* 15, 4; cf. ST II-II 153, 5). The first four refer to the undermining of prudence, the rest are contrary either to charity or divine hope.

When it comes to prudence, a person has "to judge rightly about the end" which is overcome by sheer blindness. The second act of prudence is undermined by a wilful lustful desire because one takes little time or no time to think through the consequences of one's actions. The third act occurs when a "person is inclined to consent rashly without waiting for the judgment of reason." And the final act of command is likewise impeded by wilful lust insofar as a person does not remain steadfast in his decision making and becomes inconstant (*De Malo* 15, 4).

Self-love presents a modern difficulty which Thomas anticipated (ST I-II 77, 4 obj. 1) namely, what's wrong with it if we are commanded by God to love our neighbor as ourselves (Lv 19:18)?

So, the objection would conclude by asserting that self-love cannot be a bad outcome of lust. He responds:

> The proper and essential cause of sin is to be considered on the part of the adherence to a mutable good. In this respect, every sinful act proceeds from an inordinate desire for some temporal good. Now the fact that anyone desires a temporal good inordinately is due to the fact that he loves himself inordinately; for to wish anyone some good is to love him. Therefore it is evident that inordinate love of self is the cause of every sin (ST I-II 77, 4).

So the affirmed disordered desire for sexual pleasure that lust clings to is only a mutable and apparent good. Of itself, this desire, when willed, necessarily pulls someone away from God rendering the action, whether interior or exterior, objectively sinful by reason of its moral object. It is only known by revelation that any lust-filled act undermines a participation in sanctifying grace which pulls apart our relationships with God. Likewise, common sense suggests and pastoral practice discovers that plunging into sexual sins leads one to seek self, be preoccupied with self and judge relationships in terms of what will be gained for self, namely sexual pleasure. When young couples are said to "be in love," quite often it means each loves the self before the other because each prefers personal pleasure to the true needs of the other.

Hatred of God emerges from sexual vice only because it is

clear and evident that justice demands that these sins be punished, and so one withdraws from a God who looks upon these sins as an offense against himself. By a punitive command of divine law, he seemingly takes away pleasure which human nature unreasonably demands from time to time. This is perceived as a threat from God, possibly leading someone to withdraw from him altogether. Furthermore, it leads to thinking happiness is found here on earth alone, since sexual pleasure becomes an end superseding all other ends including God. At a certain point, despair may occur about the future life of happiness with God, unless one is already sinning by presumption, that is, thinking God will reward someone regardless of what he does. In other words, the consented vice of lust attacks and undermines, ever so slowly, the theological virtues of faith and hope as it becomes rooted in one's soul precisely as a vice, rather than simply a fall into weakness. It is one thing to sin because one is weak but still struggling, and another to sin from the sheer delight of sinning, with the ensuing outcomes of the vice of lust here discussed.

Strategies to Undermine Carnal Temptations

In the case of the other vices, to overcome them takes simple meditation, contemplation, self-examination, a turning of one's will toward God in prayer, and, not giving way to false sorrows or desires. This involves struggling against certain false emotions. With food and drink, it requires some decisions to eat and drink not according to desires of pleasure, but according to true need, which takes some honest discerning rather than rationalizing.

When it comes to lust, a more serious and defensive strategy is necessary, if someone is to live the chaste lifestyle either as a consecrated person or as a single lay person. Quite often people with serious trials of lust assume that a large dose of prayer is the answer to this problem. Other than great saints whose temptations were intensely diabolical, for ordinary persons profound prayer at the time of temptations only intensifies the desire for sexual expression. This is because the intensity of the praying creates more anxiety or sorrow. With sexual temptations, one has to learn how to withdraw from them rather than fight them head on. In our book *Christian Totality: Theology of Consecrated Life*, Paul Conner, O.P., and I provide some strategies for that which everyone can find helpful to grow in chastity during bouts of temptation so as not to be overtaken by what Thomas called "the strongest desire for pleasure we have."

When one is tempted by lust, the first strategy for ordinary people is to assume it is not diabolical but from "infected" fallen nature. One has to learn how to flee from these imaginings and memories. Remaining calm and not panicking, we should believe that with Christ's grace, these inclinations can be overcome, and then we should say a firm "no" to them to break the mesmerizing effects of lustful temptation. After a very short prayer, perhaps using the name of Jesus or Mary, we then turn to something that will distract our minds such as a quick walk, putting on some classical music, playing a computer game, listening to a talk-show host we may even disagree with, or just simply reading from a book out loud. If we still have some heightened or excess energy, then it might be good to do something more creative like writing a homily, a letter, or something related to a hobby.[3] In other words, before temptations take hold of us, we have to have a plan of action, a defense learned from past sins or mistakes in this area so that we are not overcome with surprise impulses from our fallen nature. These impulses are called by Augustine and Thomas the first movements or inflammations of sin. Quite often human nature is fatigued by mental work, or loneliness, criticisms from superiors or supervisors, or even humiliating failure of some kind. The result of these negative experiences leads nature to yearn for pleasure to ameliorate the

---

[3]   Basil Cole, O.P. and Paul Conner, O.P., *Christian Totality: Theology of Consecrated Life* (Staten Island, NY: Alba House, 1997), pp. 93-96.

problem of this emptiness of spirit. Aquinas himself recognized that lack of spiritual pleasures leads one to seek after carnal pleasures (ST II-II 142, 2).

However, everyone also needs a long term strategy or lifestyle to create a favorable atmosphere for growing in chastity. Spiritual theology goes further and calls this "a plan of life." While it cannot be as orderly as a monk's horarium that marks out the times for his duties, some scheduling of a day and a week can be very helpful. Here is a short list we devised which can be helpful to the busiest of persons:

a. The cultivation of contemplation of God as well as a realistic devotion to Our Lady and the saints.

b. Regular prayer for growth in chastity in times when one is not tempted.

c. The sincere and frequent reception of the sacraments of Reconciliation and Eucharist.

d. The effort to speak frankly with one's confessor or spiritual director.

e. The avoidance of friendship based mainly on sensuality and sentiment, and the cultivation of friendships based on cultural and spiritual interests.

f. An asceticism regarding food, drink and entertainment which leads to a healthy mastery of one's mind and heart, imagination and memory, emotions and instincts (*Vita Consecrata*, 88, John Paul II).

g. A moderate love of the arts, recreation and hobbies.

h. Genuine modesty in matters of dress and behavior — without becoming prudish.[4]

---

[4] Cole and Conner, *Christian Totality*, p. 97.

Conclusion

When a culture is corroding from within, it is normally caused by a deviation from chaste sexuality. History does repeat itself. When populations are in decline, they have little energy to focus on the important and necessary values which are worth striving for. To concentrate on one's duties, it takes a strong and clear mind to discover new ways of doing things or making things. It also requires diligence, persistence and much patience with failures to keep striving for certain goals. But, with the devaluation of purity and chastity, people want their commitments and projects to succeed immediately, being used to having immediate pleasure at their beck and call. It is chastity that helps one see that certain goods are not immediately within our grasp but demand sacrifice and diligent perseverance. This is, in an exceptionally difficult way, part of the priest's vocation: to think and plan for the long term and not to become "fed up" with human stupidity on any level. To this end, celibacy or celibate love plays a key role in trying to prevent a world from self-imploding. The priest may not succeed in saving the world, but he will change himself.

Chapter Thirteen

Anger: Another Psychological Slavery of the Capital Vices

Unique to the problem of anger in the life of the priest, unlike the case with other vices, is that both anger and some of its daughter vices can sometimes become virtues. This at first blush seems contradictory. No initial formation program in the seminary or novitiate can bring the virtues which penetrate and elevate anger to a virtuous condition, for these strengths of soul can only be "won" or put into place by one's own daily efforts in a long struggle with the help of God's grace. It is well known and cited by scholars that St. Francis de Sales, the saint of mildness, once said that it took him twenty years to master his anger!

False Guilt

One of the more difficult questions that confronts the theologian on the theoretical level and the priest in his spiritual life is the paradox of anger. Some people who are very spiritual think that anger is never something morally good, yet they know that the emotion is part of the human make-up given by an all-good God. Since it often flares up and is expressed excessively, one may ask, how can it be morally good?

Good people tend to think that all anger is sinful in part because some feel guilt motivated by Christ's words, "Turn the other cheek" (Mt 5:39). In the tradition these words are a counsel not a commandment or precept; however, they are often falsely understood to be one. It is important for Catholic thought that clarity reigns on this matter, especially when the question of public defamation is involved. Thomas, after quoting Augustine on sustaining verbal injuries, clarifies the teaching on turning the other cheek:

> He says that a man should be ready to do this, if and as the occasion arises, without needing to go about doing this all the time, since even the Lord did not do this; what John reports is that when he was struck he asked, *Why do you strike me?* And we have to apply the same principle to defamatory words uttered against us, for we have to be ready to endure defamatory remarks when that seems the fitting thing to do.

> There are, however, occasions when we have to stand up to people who defame us, and these are principally twofold. In the first place, we should answer back for the sake of the person who utters the defamatory remark, in order to restrain his effrontery and further attempt to act in a similar fashion, in the spirit of Proverbs, *Answer a fool according to his folly, lest he be wise in his own eyes.* And we should in the second place answer back for the sake of larger numbers of people whose progress may be held up by our being defamed (ST II-II 72, 3).

In the answer to the first objection, Thomas further explains how this is to be done:

> One ought to restrain a defamer in a controlled sort of way; that is to say, one ought to be motivated by charity and not by the desire for self-aggrandizement.

Sometimes out of charity and not selfishness a priest needs verbal restraint to silence someone who is insulting him. At other times, using self-constraint, he needs to endure insults and verbal attacks. It takes experience together with the virtue of prudence to know when and how to respond.

Others experience guilt when they are angry because virtuous people generally do not like to inflict their anger on others and if they must, they feel a certain sadness (ST I-II 46, 2). To others of a gentle disposition, anger seems sinful because one has sometimes to inflict an evil on someone (harsh words for example and even blows in self-defense) and at times its expression is more intense than it needs to be. Because some injustices may be remembered for a long time, meditating or contemplating God's nature or Christ's life as well as vocal or contemplative prayer, can become very difficult. This can lead one to think that a lack of concentration and fervor of religious devotion is caused by a sin. Others equate the virtue of meekness or gentleness with love of neighbor and when they have to defend an important value or strike back against a neighbor, it seems to them unloving and therefore sinful. This is why Thomas speaks of the sin of negligence in this area: someone who should be angry does not become angered (ST II-II 158, 8). Finally, when looking at the emotion as such, moral "evil may be present because there is too much feeling or too little" (ST II-II 156, 1).

When someone should be angry and when not, and how strong the response should be, is really the basis for distinguishing anger as a capital vice or a reasonable and virtuous thing. While there is no such thing as a holy virtue of vainglory or lust, there can be a holy envy in the sense of wanting to be like another in his possession of a particular virtue. Anger is paradoxical: it can be holy when it is the expression of true vengeance, which on the surface of things seems like a contradiction in terms, and it can be sinful when it leads to some sinful effects including three specific vices: quarreling, contumely and blasphemy as we shall see.

Anger as an Emotion

To appreciate St. Thomas Aquinas' analysis of the question of anger, again it is necessary to examine anger (1) as an emotion, (2) as a virtue, and (3) as a vice. While it requires the spirit of temperance to "temper" the movement of wrath, which all experience, it must also be organized by a sense of justice, as will be shown.

Aquinas' distinction of the sensible appetite of the human person into the concupiscent and irascible movements is helpful. The same appetite can also be split into the impulsive or contending emotions in the face of goods and evils. The impulsive emotions go after what is pleasing to them and easily obtainable, and the contending ones go after more difficult goods and struggle against difficult evils to overcome them in order to achieve a certain good. Anger, being a defensive emotion, is very complex.

We encounter Thomas' treatment of the nature, cause, remedies and effects of anger in *Summa Theologiae* I-II 46. He begins his analysis by stating that anger is "aroused by the concourse of several emotions. Thus an angry reaction arises only when one has endured some pain, and desires and hopes for revenge. Aristotle says, *the angry man hopes to inflict punishment; he wants to be able to avenge himself. Hence if the person who has done the injury be one of very high station, the reaction will be sadness and not anger*, as Avicenna remarks" (I-II 46, 2). So being a complex emotion, certain conditions will be necessary for the act of striking back to be reasonable. But the emotion itself is both agreeable and disagreeable: revenge is sought and hoped for which is a pleasurable good, and the "opponent and assailant" is the one who is "disagreeable." This outcome requires sustained effort and energy for its achievement, which flows from the emotion. Some people, however, confuse anger with hatred which simply wishes evil on another for its own sake. Vengeance is altogether a different motive which in a puzzling way can be either good or bad.

Perceived Injustice as a Cause of Anger

What causes anger is objectively undeserved contempt, sometimes called a slight (ST I-II 47, 4). But this is something very personal because "we regard as our good what is of intense interest to us. When it is held in contempt, therefore, we feel that we ourselves are despised and we conclude that we have been offended" (I-II 47, 1 ad 3). Here is where subjective character enters into the picture. If someone has an inflated idea of himself, and his accomplishments or sensitivities get criticized, then depending upon his virtuous disposition, his anger emerges quickly, deeply or lightly, or not at all. As Thomas explains about persons filled with pride:

> ...they also become angry more easily in so far as they think that anything that is done against their will is worthless (II-II 72, 4 ad 1).

But people not necessarily lacking of virtue, such as the feeble-minded or the debilitated, can also feel unjustly slighted for other reasons:

> Defects, then, are especially painful because those who suffer from them are more easily hurt. This is the reason why men who are weak or have other shortcomings are more readily angered; they are more vulnerable (ST I-II 47, 3).

Humility and Anger

If, on the contrary, someone has a humble idea of himself, then criticisms leveled against him are taken in stride and sometimes even agreed with. The causes of any angry reaction result from being "slighted either by contempt, spite, keeping a man from having his will, and insolence" (I-II 47, 2). Thomas will also put it in another way when he says, "All the things we value we look upon as contributing to our dignity; therefore, in that it derogates from our dignity, injury done to us we regard as a slight" (I-II 47, 2). In some way the "only motive for anger, clearly, is painful injury" (I-II 47, 3). Heroic humility can lead someone to believe that he deserves the undeserved injustices inflicted upon him because of his past sins. Many saints lived this way.

Unwillful Injuries Inflicted Upon Someone

Thomas continues and says that injury can be inflicted by someone out of ignorance, emotional upset or deliberate intent. If done out of the first two, then there can be no anger or only slight anger; but, when the injury is judged to be done deliberately, one's anger becomes intense (I-II 47, 3). However, he is speaking from a very formal point of view. When married people get into arguments, quite often words slip out which are not meant to be said but are interpreted to be a major slight when they are from weakness. In his section on detraction, Aquinas has the following to say when sins of speech flow from weakness or heedlessness: "Sins of speech are of less importance insofar as they slip out so readily without premeditation" (II-II 73, 3).

Anger Is Not Always Sinful

Concerning the vice of wrath, in *Summa Theologiae* II-II 158, 1-8, Thomas raises the standard objections to show that anger is always sinful. However, in his overall treatment he will show when it is wrong and also when it can be virtuous. In the objections to article one of this question he lays out the usual scripture quotations suggesting that wrath is always sinful: "Whoever is angry with his brother shall be liable to judgment" (Mt

5:22), and "thou shalt not hate thy brother in thy heart" (Lv 19:17). The solution will be found in the "sed contra" of the article with a quotation from Chrysostom:

> *[A] man who is angry without cause,* he says, *is guilty, but not he that is angry with cause, for without anger sound doctrine would not be advanced or good judgment maintained or crime put down.* So then to be angry is not always wrong (ST II-II 158, 1).

He goes on to develop the idea that anger can sometimes rise up before reason enters in and perhaps drags it down. It may also follow the direction of reason in attacking something vicious which is called "anger through zeal" (II-II 158, 1 ad 2). This latter kind of anger can blur reason but not blind it. Nevertheless, he concludes by saying with Gregory the Great, "Let anger stand up robustly against vice… like the bodyguard of reason" (II-II 158, 1 ad 4). Anger is good when ruled by reason and bad when it expels reason (II-II 158, 2). What makes its object good is that it seeks to punish with the right intention for the correction of fault and the order of justice without its inflection being immoderately fierce (Ibid.). He does not seek to punish someone for the sake of inflicting an evil as such (II-II 158, 2 ad 2). Thomas is convinced throughout his writings that human nature is made to express reasonable anger to defend self and very important objective values. In that sense, it can be both a reaction to insult and injury and, as circumstances dictate and prudence motivates, a determined effort to do something ultimately helpful for others which may mean inflicting retaliation on them. The difficulty in the priesthood is that one may reasonably use anger to solve a problem, but often it only creates more problems causing some bad people to become worse and discouraging good people from becoming better. It requires deep prudence when and how to express it and when to refrain from it.

Anger as a Capital Vice

Anger is called a capital vice, because when seen as anger expressed merely from passion and not from right reason, it becomes a major source of inordinate deeds (II-II 158, 6). There are six daughters to this vice traditionally enumerated by Gregory the Great: quarreling, swelled head, contumely, clamor, indignation and blasphemy (II-II 158, 7). Thomas' thoughts on these outcomes can speak for themselves:

> Wrath can be taken at three stages, of thought, word, and deed. As conceived in the heart, it gives birth to two vices. One regards the person with whom you are angry because you hold that it was unworthy of him to act as he did towards you; this is called indignation. The other regards the person who is angry in that he hatches up various plans for getting his revenge and broods over them. This, which is called a swollen spirit, is referred to in *Job, Will a wise man fill his belly with hot wind.*
>
> Next, anger in speech, and here also there are two disorders. One as regards the manner of speech; and this… is displayed by a man who says to his brother, *Racha!*; it is called clamor which signifies noisy and confused speech. The other is bursting out into offensive words, and this is called blasphemy, when they are against God, and contumely, when against our neighbor.
>
> Lastly anger in deed, and so anger gives rise to quarreling, which we take to man all wrathful behavior which is injurious to our neighbor (ST II-II 158, 7).

With four of these daughters, he gives no analysis since they seem to be evident from experience or as explained in the body of the article. However, quarreling, contumely, and blasphemy need more treatment, which Aquinas offers in different places in his

Summa. They pertain largely to sins of speech and this requires further explication. Quarreling is the least offensive vice and blaspheming the most serious.

Quarreling, Contumely and Blasphemy

Quarreling, which not only can spring from anger but also from causal vices, is done by "someone contradicting the statement of another" (II-II 116, 1). It can be directed against a person out of a simple lack of love "that should make men one in spirit" (Ibid.). Discord and contention would occasionally fall into this category. However, some people have "no hesitancy about being disagreeable to the person speaking" which is "counter to friendliness or affability that is concerned with agreeableness in human relations." This shows a certain contempt of the person, when done with that intention, and is why it is related to the sin of wrath (II-II 116, 2 ad 3).

Ridicule (sometimes called derision or mockery) has the intention to inflict private or public embarrassment on another, which also happens when someone is defamed or slandered against. The aim of the ridiculer is different, however, as it is his aim to make someone confused or feel disturbed by making fun of his seeming defects. This is a form of contempt and takes away a person's tranquillity or spirit of peace (II-II 75, 1). Thomas gives no evident examples here, but these acts of humiliation can be done by teachers to students, bishops to priests, superiors to subjects, priests to people, supervisors to workers and men to women, women to men, nurses to people who may be senile or in dementia. It is a form of manipulation to dominate people or relieve frustration. All things being equal, it is different from a Marine sergeant ridiculing those in boot camp because he intends something radically different, namely, preparing them to fight in a war.

The problem of blasphemy, a sin against faith, is analyzed by our Master in the *Summa Theologiae* II-II 13, 1-4. It is the sin

which disparages the excellent goodness of God by denying something belonging to him or affirming something which is not of
God (II-II 13, 1). Here among other places, Thomas sees all of
God's attributes and his very essence under the over-arching idea
of God's perfect goodness. But to disparage this goodness is a form
of detesting God (II-II 13, 4). Reasoning about the souls in hell,
he teaches that they blaspheme God's justice because they

> ...keep a perverse will turned against God's justice, as
> being still attached to the things for which they are
> being punished, wishing to enjoy them if they could,
> and hating the punishments inflicted because of them.
> They sorrow for their past sins, not because they re-
> gret them, but because they are punished for them.
> Accordingly this detestation of divine justice is in them
> an interior blasphemy of the heart (ST II-II 13, 4).

Nevertheless in describing blasphemy, grave in its matter,
Aquinas shows when and why it is not always a mortal sin:

> Blasphemy may vent itself without deliberation in two
> ways. First, when a man does not advert to the blas-
> phemous nature of his speech; this may happen
> through a sudden movement of passion breaking out
> into words welling up in his imagination without heed
> of their meaning. This is a venial sin, and lacks the
> especial character of blasphemy. Second when he is
> aware of the significance of his words and adverts to
> the fact that they are blasphemous. In that case, he is
> not excused from mortal sin even as neither is a man
> who in a sudden gust of anger kills one who is sitting
> beside him (II-II 13, 2 ad 3).

To conclude this section, it becomes very obvious how
important the virtue of gentleness is as a defense against acting
on uncontrolled and disproportionate anger, which opens the
human person to become a slave of this passion leading to a lack

of charity and justice toward God and neighbor. For the priest, anger is an aspect of his personality that should rarely be exercised on a daily basis. Thus when it is prudently shown, it teaches and ultimately defends the people from certain evil persons and tendencies.

Virtuous Shaping of the Emotion of Anger

Now the virtues which shape the passion of anger are gentleness, vengeance and clemency. Before one begins to consider vengeance (a virtue under justice that deals with a response to injustices either according to the measure of law or the measure of prudence for private offenses), it is essential that the virtue of gentleness be examined. Gentleness (or meekness) is a certain strength although not quite the strength of courage and a difficult one to develop for certain temperaments. Gentleness has to be developed in everyone, whereas clemency, which shows mercy in punishing people, is the virtue for those in charge of a parish or a school or even a penal system which must carry out certain punishments mandated by civil or even natural law (II-II 157, 1). Gentleness moderates the emotion of anger itself and clemency moderates "the infliction of punishments" (Ibid.). Gentleness must restrain or temper the passion of anger for "we are more naturally inclined to resent an injury done to us than to let the matter slide. 'Scarcely anybody,' Sallust observes, 'counts for little an injury done to him'" (II-II 157, 2 ad 2). While thinking of clemency, Thomas in the following passage gives a fine understanding of the effect of gentleness in the clement man:

> This moderateness (in punishing) comes from a certain sweetness of feeling which abhors anything which can afflict another. Accordingly Seneca calls clemency a certain leniency of spirit. Conversely there seems to be a certain harshness of heart in one who does not blush at giving pain to others (ST II-II 157, 3 ad 1).

As one grows in this virtue of gentleness, it "renders a man composed and self-possessed" (II-II 157, 4). This perfection in turn then helps a person become a better thinker because the rush of anger frequently interferes with the mind's judgment about the truth (Ibid.). Often, when engaged in discussions with fellow priests, gentleness holds a person back from being harsh, which can sometimes make the truth of faith or reason seem unpalatable. And as we shall see, when "vengeance" has to be taken, the mind is much clearer in making this judgment when there is gentleness of spirit already there.

Virtuous Use of Aggression

How anger is legitimately expressed is the key to understanding what St. Thomas calls the virtue of vengeance. Unfortunately, the English language uses the word "vengeance" as if it were always something morally evil. For Thomas vengeance can be both morally good or morally evil depending upon the circumstances and intent. It deals with injustice and the emotion of anger which, as was seen, becomes stirred up when a "slight" or injustice is perceived. He begins his treatment with four pithy articles in the *Summa Theologiae* II-II 108.

While scripture seems to suggest that vengeance is always morally wrong, he reasons that in itself it cannot be evil or unlawful because God does it and "we should expect from God only what is good and lawful" (II-II 108, 1). His analysis begins with the idea that the intention of an avenger must be morally good and if not, then any avenging act is wrong:

> Vengeance is accomplished by some punishment being inflicted upon one who has given offense. In vengeance, therefore, the attitude of the avenger (*intentio*) must be considered. Should his intention be centered chiefly upon the evil done to the recipient and it is satisfied with that, then the act is entirely unlawful.

Taking delight in evil done to another is in fact a type of hatred, the opposite of charity with which we are bound to love all. Nor is there any excuse just because the evil is intended towards one who has himself unjustly inflicted injury, even as there is no excuse for hating someone who already hates us. A person has no right to sin against another because the other first sinned against him; this is to be overcome by evil, which St. Paul forbids, *Be not overcome by evil, but overcome evil by good* (Rm 12:21) (ST II-II 108, 1).

In the next paragraph of the same article, Thomas will then show when vengeance is virtuous and why:

Vengeance, however, can be lawful so long as all proper conditions are safeguarded — if the intention of the avenger is aimed chiefly at a good to be achieved by punishing the wrongdoer; thus, for example, at the correction of the wrongdoer, or at least at restraining him and relieving others; at safeguarding the right (*justitiae*) and honor to God (Ibid.).

This exercise of vengeance does **not** imply the overthrow of patience "in sustaining wrongs done" to self "personally" within due limits with regard to turning the other cheek, because it is another virtue for a different situation. Patience may not be called for in "allowing wrongs against God or neighbor" (II-II 108, 1 ad 1). Thomas then really sums up a defense of vengeance as a virtue by citing Cicero's insight that "by vengeance we resist force and wrong and in general anything sinister (i.e. hostile) either by self-defense or by retaliating" (II-II 108, 2). Essentially the virtue of vengeance comes down to its purpose, namely "to check evil" (II-II 108, 4). Now one can fail in this virtue by going to extremes either by cruelty or ferocity against persons or failing to "inflict punishment at all," and he cites Proverbs: *He that spares the rod spoils the child* (II-II 108, 4 ad 3). Of course, the example limps pastorally speaking in light of contemporary concerns about the role of punishing one's children, but that concern should lead to further discussion to make certain that cruelty and harm to children are avoided.

Application of the Teaching for Priests

No one lives through his priesthood without feeling the emotion of anger. Many daily routines eventually get to the priest, especially when he is tired, lonely, or discouraged. At these times he is vulnerable to becoming angry with himself or his people because of discouraging results and to expressing his anger in unfitting ways, producing no fruits of change. Being an image of Christ to people is not easy since he must learn to deal with different temperaments among his flock and his fellow priests who may have their own ideas about evangelization which disagree with his. The more attached he is to his own methods and ideas, the less able he is to accept different points of view. Attacking, criticizing or disagreeing even pleasantly with his parishioners or fellow priests can often lead to an explosion: "To attack something I consider of value is in some way to attack me!" Beginners in the spiritual life are simply that way. So, the priest has to cultivate a love of gentleness while not becoming a wimp in the face of evils in his parish community. Even with the help of grace, it is difficult; and without grace, impossible.

The priest faces people in different modes: the pulpit, the confessional, the classroom, the parlor, meetings, picnics, and other social events. In the pulpit, he may be able to express his anger at sin, but in other places he may find that holding it back is best based on the adage that "honey attracts the flies more than vinegar." Feeling anger is not a sin, but expressing it in the external forum requires prudence as to when, how, where, for how long and for what reason. Only the gentle person will be able to understand truly the answers to these questions. This requires uncommon restraint, if not, sometimes, heroic virtue.

Chapter Fourteen

Acedia, A Forgotten Capital Vice

The most neglected capital vice in the literature of spiritual theology in our times is acedia.[1] This study is written especially for priests who must deal with acedia both in the confessional as well as in their personal lives. However, little attention is paid to the problem of acedia so that quite often, priests do not know how to interpret certain key signs of this vice. Acedia is often simply defined as laziness or sloth. The translation I will use is "spiritual apathy," and yet it is something more than mere boredom with prayer, study, and the sacraments. For as we shall see, acedia is a running away from God due to sadness.

This vice was discussed quite prominently in Cassian's writings for monks, so much so, perhaps, that it came to be seen primarily as a sin among religious. This is simply false. Perhaps also sadness or negativity came to be understood by many other authors as a sin even in the case of reasonable sadness. This too is not on the mark. On the contrary, some types of sadness are legitimate and morally upright since they result from trials like the dark nights of the soul or simply the sadness of losing a son or a daughter, or the receiving of a new assignment which is repugnant to one's wishes. However, it appears in the early literature of the Church as though sadness and acedia were undiffer-

---

[1] I owe a debt of gratitude to Urban Voll's lectorate thesis entitled *The Vice of Acedia* submitted to the Pontifical Faculty of the Dominican House of Studies in 1950. The lectorate was a degree peculiar to the Dominican Order and gave one the right to teach in any House of Studies in the Order of Preachers.

entiated when in fact the sadness that comes with the pressure of fasting and praying, or the apostolate would be normal outcomes rather than sins. Nevertheless, such trials could lead someone to the crossroad of sin or the exercise of virtue in order to relieve sadness. Thomas Aquinas is very clear in this regard when he says that "the despondency involved here — not the vice of acedia arising from whatever cause — is not a distinct vice simply because it makes a man shirk a heavy and burdensome work or sad for any cause whatever. (Acedia) is special because he is sad about **the divine good**. It is this which is of the essence of spiritual apathy, which seeks **wrongful relaxation** in so far as it spurns good" (ST II-II 35, 4 ad 3). Many clergy and laity may very well be caught in the grip of certain sexual vices or even drunkenness because of this capital vice of acedia and not understand that acedia is their problem. When the trials of life seem to be overwhelming, it is very difficult to love God since he seems to have abandoned us. If we harbor such thoughts, eventually the temptation to run away from God into other sins, out of anger or discouragement with God, becomes quite powerful since our love for him is often based on consolations and other considerations. To those in the grip of acedia trials seem like undeserved punishments from God.

The Teaching of the Church on Acedia

The *Catechism of the Catholic Church* actually has several paragraphs based on the writings of Cassian and other monastic writers without going into the particular analysis of St. Thomas Aquinas. There are three places where the *Catechism* speaks of acedia. The first citation includes it with other sins against God's love:

> 2094. One can sin against God's love in various ways:
> - *indifference* neglects or refuses to reflect on divine charity; it fails to consider its prevenient goodness and denies its power.

- *ingratitude* fails or refuses to acknowledge divine charity and to return him love for love.
- *lukewarmness* is hesitation or negligence in responding to divine love; it can imply refusal to give oneself over to the prompting of charity.
- *acedia* or spiritual sloth **goes so far as** to refuse the joy that comes from God and **to be repelled by divine goodness**.
- *hatred of God* comes from pride. It is contrary to love of God, whose goodness it denies, and whom it presumes to curse as the one who forbids sins and inflicts punishments.

Here in number 2094, acedia is identified with spiritual sloth. However, in number 2733, acedia is called an effect of presumption:

> 2733. Another temptation, to which presumption opens the gate, is acedia. The spiritual writers understand by this **a form of depression due to lax ascetical practice, decreasing vigilance, carelessness of heart**. "The spirit indeed is willing, but the flesh is weak." The greater the height, the harder the fall. Painful as discouragement is, it is the reverse of presumption. The humble are not surprised by their distress; it leads them to trust more, to hold fast in constancy.

Additionally, in number 2755, acedia is called a form of depression or sadness which comes about from a lack of ascetical practice:

> 2755. Two frequent temptations threaten prayer: lack of faith and acedia — a form of depression stemming from lax ascetical practice that leads to discouragement.

A Need to Synthesize and Explain the Meaning of the *Catechism* on Acedia

While a Thomistic analysis will not say that the statements in these sections are false, it will re-order some of the concepts in order to bring about a clearer synthesis in explaining this complex vice than we find here in the sections quoted from the *Catechism*.

Because of a lack of interest in this vice (especially among moralists who are interested more in virtues than vices), many thinkers have called this problem of acedia simply sloth or laziness. Sloth, physical or spiritual, is indeed one effect of this vice, so the *Catechism* is not at all off the mark. St. Thomas in his work *On Evil* (*De Malo*) goes into the question of acedia at greater length than in the *Summa Theologiae* and explains that this vice is more complicated than what either Cassian or others have said about it. And, although he followed St. Gregory the Great's list for the capital vices, he changes Gregory's terminology from "sadness" to "acedia". Perhaps this is because he used Cassian's writings for his spiritual reading as did St. Dominic himself. In his writings Cassian often speaks of acedia conflating some sadness with a sin or the first movements of a sin. But the theologian needs to search out the issue: if sorrow or sadness or a form of depression is an emotion (which is neither intrinsically evil nor morally good as such), how can sadness be a sin? The *Catechism* agrees with Thomas' perspective when it says in number 1767:

> In themselves passions are neither good nor evil. They are morally qualified only to the extent that they effectively engage reason and will. Passions are said to be voluntary, "either because they are commanded by the will or because the will does not place obstacles in their way." [STh I-II, 24, 1 corp. art.]. It belongs to the perfection of the moral or human good that the passions be governed by reason [St. Thomas Aquinas, STh I-II, 24, 3].

Aquinas raises the same objection:

> (John) Damascene takes acedia to be a species of sadness, which is one of the four passions. But passions are not sins, because we are neither praised nor blamed for them. Therefore acedia is not a sin (*De Malo* 11, 1 obj. 8).

In the *Summa*, he gives a clear response to the objection:

> Damascene teaches that spiritual apathy is a *kind of oppressive sorrow*, which so depresses a man that he wants to do nothing.... Spiritual apathy implies then a certain weariness about work. We known this from a gloss... that it is a *torpor of the mind which cannot face getting down to work* (ST II-II 35, 1).

> Such sorrow is always bad. Sometimes it is bad in itself, sometimes in its effects. It is bad in itself when it arises from an apparent evil which truly is a good, just as that delight arising from an apparent good which truly is an evil is bad. Since, then, a spiritual good is a real good, the sorrowing over it is bad in itself. It is bad in its effects when the object is really bad but so oppresses a man that it drags him away from good work. Thus the Apostle does not want a penitent man *to be absorbed by too much sorrow*. Since, then, spiritual apathy as we are using it here denotes sorrow over spiritual things, it is doubly evil, both in itself and in its effects and so is a sin (II-II 35, 4 ad 3).

The nuance of a particular form of sadness which attaches to this vice is also suggested when Thomas says angels cannot have it (I 13, 2 ad 1), nor the vice of gluttony nor lust, since they have no body for these passions or emotions. Yet, acedia is akin to the sadness of envy insofar as it causes one's soul to hurt. And while the *Catechism* teaches that it may be "due to lax ascetical practice, decreasing vigilance, carelessness of heart," it may also be due to other causes and sins as well. Moreover, the *Catechism* does not explain how "acedia or spiritual sloth goes so far as to refuse the joy that comes from God and to be repelled by divine goodness" nor why or how this "feeling" of refusal can become a sin. Additionally one might ask: If it is refusal, then is acedia not really a fear rather than a sadness? What does it mean to refuse "joy" coming from God and how can someone be repelled by divine goodness? It is important to keep in mind that the *Catechism* is not in error, but it needs to be complemented and completed by the science of moral theology either in the Thomistic vein or that of other theological schools.

The Passion of Sorrow: A Thomistic Perspective

St. Thomas treats the passions or emotions as bodily and by analogy intellectual movements in the face of sensible or imagined goods or evils. Sadness of the body is called *dolor*, and sadness of the soul is called *tristitia*. Fasting can cause sadness to the body because one takes upon himself the pain of hunger; however, this can in turn become a sadness of soul if one becomes impatient or expresses discomfort because of the past sin of gluttony and the present unfulfilled desire for food. Enduring injustice can also cause sadness of soul. A physical infirmity, for example a broken bone, can cause both bodily and spiritual sorrow, the latter being the effect of hating this cross. Further, sadness can also exist when that which is objectively good is seen to be evil; one, therefore, flees from a real good seen as an apparent evil, namely God's life in our soul. Sin is usually defined as a choice of an apparent good, but fleeing from an apparent evil when in fact it is a real good also means that one seeks an apparent good in turning or fleeing a real good. This indeed is complex.

In the case of illicit physical pleasures, one has to learn to run away from them. However, in the case of real goods for the soul that appear to be evil (such as being faithful to one's spouse or one's priesthood in difficult times), one has to learn to resist and not to run away from the toil of achieving certain goods. This is where the potential parts of the virtue of fortitude enters, such as patience, long-suffering and perseverance protecting charity's presence in the soul. And it is here where we begin to understand the moral evil of acedia which is not merely a feeling but a consented sin of sorrow connected with one's relationship to God.

In Thomistic theological literature acedia is a specific kind of sorrow, a deadly sin implying spiritual apathy, disgust with spiritual things, boredom or a kind of grieving over what is good for the human person, thus seeing and feeling as if it were really evil. As an oppressive sorrow, it is both physical and volitional. When we are in pain or sorrow, we want to get away from what is causing it because human nature is made for delight. Since Thomas did not know psychiatric depression as we do today, he tends to think that humans are responsible for such states of sadness resulting in the inability to act (ST I-II 135, 8). Fear resembles acedia but it is distinct. Fear often comes about because a man sees physical toil as a future burden to his nature and flees from it (I-II 41, 4), whereas acedia so weighs upon the soul that a man wants to do almost nothing, at least for a time. But why is acedia a sin?

A True Good Looked Upon as an Evil to be Avoided

Turning inordinately by choice from a true good when obligatory is a general way of describing the sin of acedia, for it allows an excessive sorrow to exist in the soul (ST II-II 35, 1; *De Malo* 11, 10). Thomas also offers an example of someone who could become so penitential that he becomes unable to do good works, which would be imprudent. This does not yet mean that a reasonable sorrow has become the special sin of acedia. For it to be a special sin, the sadness has to be about a spiritual good looked upon by the intellect as an evil to be avoided. That is, this particular moral evil is sadness over the very spiritual good itself. It is not the same as a carnal vice which can pursue bodily comfort and pleasure so much that a person shrinks from work or labor (ST II-II 35, 2), for slothfulness can be the outcome of carnal vices as well, not simply of acedia. This is why "sloth" is not a good translation for acedia. To be sad about the virtues, specifically or generally, is not what acedia is about either, but rather "to be sorrowful about the divine good, which charity rejoices in…" (II-II 35, 2). This is why the *Catechism* places acedia as a sin against God. Thomas further describes it as "the horror, the loathing of the divine good due to flesh's utter victory over the spirit…" (II-II 35, 3). He further describes it in the following way:

> Spiritual apathy is not mentally running away from any spiritual good you can think of, but **from the divine good** to which we should cleave. Thus if a man suffers because someone forces him to do virtuous acts he is not bound to do, that is not the sin of spiritual apathy. It is only spiritual apathy when it involves having to do something for God (emphasis added) (ST II-II 35, 3 ad 2).

The Sin of Acedia Voluntarily Blocking Divine Joy

Joy as an after-glow of charity rejoices in the goodness of God himself and secondarily in the soul's participation in the divine good. Acedia, however, undermines that joy, especially since it induces boredom or sadness with regard to religious things — from prayers to receiving the sacraments especially when obligatory. However, it is one thing to be lukewarm and do spiritual works in a careless way and another not to do them at all. However, the latter is not yet hatred of God which is opposed to his goodness or joy as such. Rather, acedia is rejecting a more personal good from God, such as sanctifying grace, which is meant to be our own, and causing us to feel sad about it. The reason why we feel sadness about such great a good as grace is because it will undermine our judgments concerning happiness and the purpose of life. God and his goodness can seem to us to be evil when we determine that heavy difficulties will ensue should we go to confession or pray or attempt to go to Mass or give up specific sins and live according to God's will. These difficulties are seen to be insurmountable because a person does not want to change his life. As Thomas puts it:

> Now this divine good is saddening to man on account of the opposition of the spirit with the flesh because as the Apostle says in Galatians 5:17, "The flesh lusts against the spirit"; and therefore when love of the flesh is dominant in man he loathes spiritual good as if something contrary to himself, just as a man with embittered taste finds wholesome food distasteful and is grieved whenever he has to take such food. Therefore such distress and distaste or disgust (tedium) about spiritual and divine good is acedia, which is a special sin (*De Malo* 11, 3).

Why Would Someone Want to Resist Being Joyful?

Looking at number 2034 of the *Catechism*, we read that "acedia or spiritual sloth goes so far as to refuse the joy that comes from God and to be repelled by divine goodness." Thomas posits two possible objections that seem to contradict this:

> Every mortal sin is contrary to a precept of God. But acedia does not seem to be contrary to any precept, for no precept about joy is included among the Ten Commandments. Therefore acedia is not a mortal sin.

Every mortal sin is contrary to the spiritual life. However, it does not necessarily pertain to the spiritual life that a person works joyfully but it suffices the he does the work; otherwise whoever would do a work he is obliged to do, if he were not to find joy in it, would sin mortally. Therefore acedia is not a mortal sin (*De Malo* 11, 3 objs. 2 & 7).

In his reply to these arguments, Thomas states that since acedia is "repugnance of the human affections to a spiritual divine good [which in this case is sanctifying grace and the infused virtue of charity]; indeed such repugnance is obviously contrary to charity, which adheres to a divine good and **rejoices in it**..." (my emphasis) (*De Malo* 11, 3). The answers to the objections then are quite simple. To the first objection he says that the third commandment is *de facto* fulfilled when the repose of the mind in God is done accordingly through prayer and meditation (*De Malo* 11, 3 ad 2). Later in the article, he also reminds us in the answers to the sixth and seventh objection that joy "does fall under a precept, just as that man should love God because joy follows upon love (*De Malo* 11, 3 ad 6); "the joy which arises from charity, to which acedia is opposed, necessarily belongs to spiritual life, as does charity itself, and for this reason acedia is a mortal sin" (*De Malo* 11, 3 ad 7).

Acedia, then, is opposed to joy because on the natural level both joy and sadness have as their origin the emotion of love but in opposite ways. In the case of adhering to sadness, one cleaves to the goods of this world inordinately. On the other hand, if one loves God, then one resists the sadness and surrenders to God's offer of grace. In his treatment of joy, the Master shows us why charity is related to joy when he writes:

Charity, however, is love of God, and God's good is something fixed and unchangeable, for he himself is his own goodness. Moreover, the very fact that he is loved, means that he is in the one who loves him, by reason of the noblest of his effects, indicated in 1 John, *He who abides in love, abides in God and God abides in him.* The spiritual joy that comes from God, then, is the effect of charity (ST II-II 28, 2).

Nevertheless, joy is not a virtue as such despite Paul's command to the Philippians to "Rejoice in the Lord always" (Ph 4:4). Joy cannot be a virtue distinct from charity since the virtue which "inclines us to love some good, to desire it and to rejoice in it is the same" (II-II 28, 4). Joy then is a "certain act or effect of charity. On this account it is numbered among what St. Paul in Galatians calls *the fruits of the Spirit*" (Ibid.).

The Daughters of Acedia

At first, acedia might not seem to be a capital vice that motivates other vices. Thomas shows the contrary by first raising the objection that it is not a capital vice because it does not "move a person to other sinful acts [but] rather it immobilizes a person; for it is an oppressive sadness, as Damascene says" (*De Malo* 11 obj. 2). Therefore, it would follow that it cannot be a sin. He then brilliantly answers the objection by arguing that "Acedia immobilizes the person subject to it as regards those things that are the cause of his sadness, but it renders its subject prompt in regard to contrary things" (*De Malo* 11 ad 2).

He further argues that acedia is indeed a capital vice for

a vice is capital which gives rise to other vices as being their final cause. Now just as men proceed to do or to avoid many things on account of the pursuit of pleasure, so also on account of flight from sadness, for both seem to be for the same reason, i.e., to seek good and flee from evil. Since then acedia is a kind of sadness about an internal divine good, as envy is concerning our neighbor's good... just as many vices arise from envy inasmuch as man does many inordinate acts to repel such sadness that results from our neighbor's good, in such a way too acedia is a capital vice (*De Malo* 11, 4).

In continuing to deal with the question of acedia's causality, he shows that its outcome is sadness over divine things. Since "no one can long endure sadness without joy," a person does two things: he flees from the "saddening things," and he turns to what will bring about pleasure (Ibid.). This can be sex, drugs or alcohol among other things. If spiritual pleasures are rejected by a person, then he goes after carnal pleasures. This primes him to pursue the daughter vices of acedia, which Thomas more clearly enumerates in the *Summa*. These he takes from the list of Gregory the Great: *malice, spite, pusillanimity, despair, sluggishness about the Commandments, straying of the mind towards illicit things* (ST II-II 35, 4 obj. 2). The last of these vices begins the moral downfall of a person by engulfing him in sensuality prompted by acedia itself. "We do many things for sorrow's sake, either to avoid it, or, exasperated by its pressure, to do something else" (II-II 35, 4). Thomas explains more fully:

> Gregory has it right when he names the offspring of spiritual apathy. Aristotle notes that *no one can remain for a long time in sorrow without some pleasure*. Now two things come from such sorrow; first, a man will disengage himself from whatever brings sorrow; second, he will go over to things that bring him pleasure. The man, for example, who cannot find joy in spiritual delights will give himself over to bodily ones, as Aristotle notes. The process of escape from sorrow is first to get away from painful things themselves, then second to fight whatever is causing them. Now spiritual goods, which spiritual apathy is all about, are both end and means. Despair flees the end; pusillanimity the means when these present difficulties involved in

following the counsels; sluggishness about the Commandments when they are matters of common justice. Resistance against the painful kind of spiritual goods sometimes turns against the men who recommend them, and this is spite; or against the goods themselves, when one is led to detest them, and that properly is malice. When someone is under pressure of this sorrow over external pleasure, then we have straying after illicit things (ST II-II 35, 4 ad 2).

Overcoming This Vice

How one avoids this debilitating vice is the pastoral problem par excellence for many priests and laity as well. Aquinas gives barely a hint but he opens up a solution that needs exploring:

> Sin must always be avoided, but we should sometimes run from and sometimes resist its onslaught. Fleeing is the answer when continual thinking about it increases the incentive to sin (as in sexual sin); hence the advice, "avoid fornication." Whereas resistance is called for when steady thought would help to remove the incentive arising from some less pressing persuasion. This is what happens with spiritual apathy, since the more we think about spiritual goods the more delightful they become to us, and spiritual apathy goes away (ST II-II 35, 2 ad 4).

It was Cassian among other writers, whose writings brought attention to the problem of disturbing thoughts producing sadness. He is cited by Aquinas in several places involving the discussion on acedia:

> Spiritual apathy greatly troubles monks at noon. It

> strikes like a recurring fever; it lays the soul low with sultry fires at regular and fixed intervals (II-II 35, 1 obj. 2).

> It arises from the fact that we groan about not having spiritual fruit and we think that other, distant monasteries are better off than ours (II-II 35, 1 obj. 3).

> …acedia is well known to the solitary and is a most troublesome and persistent foe to the hermit (II-II 35, 3 obj. 3).

However, for Thomas, these feelings are not necessarily willful sins and do not arise from the vice of acedia itself, but are simply its first movements. They are feelings of despondency caused by a monk's reflections about himself, which he must fight in order to stay the course of his vocation. In like manner, married people sometimes feel discouraged and despondent over their marriages. Germain Grisez points out that for a married couple to keep thinking of the faults and failures of the other and wishing not to be married at all or wishing that one had married another person can be a grave sin. The same could be said for clerics wanting to be free from the priesthood or their particular institute, if they are religious:

> Directly contrary to that will is any wish not be married or not to be married to this person. Even though such wishes come spontaneously to mind when marital disappointments and difficulties occur, spouses should recognize them as the primary temptation against conjugal love, and reject them as bad thoughts.…

> Intentionally to entertain such thoughts seems to be grave matter. For, although classical moralists failed to identify this kind of sin, it is clear that any married person's wish not to be married or not to be married

to his or her spouse seriously damages marital love. In fact, it is likely to lead to adultery and is certainly the first step in any attempt to dissolve a marriage by divorce. Like any other sin, of course, this one is not mortal unless, aware of a grave obligation *not* to entertain such wishes, one nevertheless chooses to do so; but even if the sin is only venial, it paves the way for infidelity and divorce.[2]

From the point of view of the priesthood or the consecrated life, such negative thoughts can enter into the mind as the result of sadness or despondency. As the thoughts gain control, loving and doing God's will becomes problematic. Consequently, prayer and contemplation begin to wane and feverish activity may take its place as a substitute for the direct love of God himself. Instead of rejoicing in God and his presence, one rejoices in one's own works and ultimately revels in oneself. Gradually the running away from God and resting in the goods of earth become the lifestyle.

The Healing of Meditation and Contemplation

Assuming a grace of reconversion, the return to or its revitalization in one's priesthood or consecrated life requires that meditation and contemplation resume a central role in the life of someone who has been caught in the web of disordered sorrow about God and running away from him into worldly goods and carnal pleasures. Thomas recalls the idea that "meditation is the cause of devotion since through meditation man conceives the idea of giving himself to the service of God" (II-II 82, 3). The reason why meditation and contemplation are crucial in

---

2   Germain Grisez, *The Way of the Lord Jesus, Living a Christian Life* (Quincy, IL: Franciscan Press, 1992), p. 620.

overcoming acedia is because they do something for the person that other activities cannot:

> Because God is most lovable, meditation upon the divine nature is in itself the strongest incentive to love and therefore to devotion. Yet because the human mind is weak, it must be led to knowledge and love of divine things through sensible objects. Chief among these sensible objects which dispose for devotion is the passion of Christ.... Hence, meditation upon matters relating to Christ's humanity readily dispose for devotion, yet the object of devotion is the divine nature (ST II-II 82, 3 ad 2).

Thinking and pondering on God produces great spiritual joy:

> Secondarily devotion is caused by considering our own weaknesses, for this consideration is the starting point from which a devout man proceeds when he trusts not in himself, but instead subjects himself to God. The results of this consideration are the opposite of the first. As one thinks of his own defects, sorrow necessarily follows, but accidentally, joy is caused because we hope for divine assistance in overcoming our weaknesses. Devotion principally and primarily, therefore, causes pleasure, but secondarily and accidentally it causes godly sorrow (II-II 82, 4).

The beginnings of acedia can thus be defeated, but this requires perseverance in meditation and contemplation. Without the essential giving of oneself to God on a daily basis, the sorrows and crosses of the priestly and religious life can swamp all the best desires, hopes, and dreams in such a way that one can be tempted to escape into darker thoughts, motives and foul actions. The problem is that we do not experience God's loving presence directly, and indeed when heavy burdens come our way, we often experience a sense of his absence or abandonment. We often give in to the false conclusion that we should abandon him as well. Consequently, when these moods and thoughts overtake us, we tend to rush headlong into sinful pleasures to relieve the sadness and tears of life's trials. But a contemplative person knows how to deal with these thoughts and counteract them by the truths of faith which contradict the negativity and erroneous concepts that can flow from bitter sorrows and from the temptations to acedia.

Postlude

The more a priest understands what his enemies are within and without, as he tries to conquer them with the help of God's grace, the easier it will become to shepherd his people in the Truth of the Catholic faith with joy in his heart. He will understand that all his people suffer, more or less, the same problems he does in varying ways. His own moments of weakness, loneliness and love of illusion which he tries to overcome is the stuff of striving for holiness that all of his flock must follow. The path to intimacy with God is a battle for excellence and freedom for virtue and a battle against an evil person (the devil) and the potential evil within himself.

I hope this book has expressed the essential strands for the main enemy lines. The tackling begins at those days of initial formation in the novitiate or seminary where the priestly candidate must learn the difference between his authentic self and the false images, projected by the seeds of the capital vices lurking within.

In his commentary on 1 Timothy, St. Thomas teaches that superiors and teachers must do all they can to restrain thinkers who teach false doctrine and prevent their charges from following the teaching of false doctrine. Since the Second Vatican Council, the radical and hidden dissent found among theologians together with the devaluation of philosophy and theology of St. Thomas have left many ordained men very vulnerable to the onslaught of those hidden enemies we have discussed in this book. When we do not know or understand the enemies in battle, we are more easily apt to succumb to their invasion and depart from the priesthood as many have since the Council.

When the solid teaching of an Aquinas (or a Bonaventure or an Augustine) is replaced by ambiguity, or simply, an absence of practical wisdom, each person's temperament tends to create its own spiritual theology and rationalize one's follies rather than allowing the hard truth to confront the inner soul and God. Instead of conforming to objective truth, one lives by subjective feelings about holiness. As a result the nature of the priestly life becomes skewed. As the priest stays away or withdraws his intellect from the common wisdom of the Church, he becomes hard and strict with people on matters that may very well be accidental and he lowers his personal standards of excellence for himself.

In this book, I hope its analysis under the tutelage of St. Thomas has alerted at least some who might realize that they are on the edge of a precipice leading to the loss of their vocation, so that they may take the steps necessary to return to the way, the truth and the life of Jesus Christ.